C-286   **CAREER EXAMINATION SERIES**

*This is your
PASSBOOK for...*

Fingerprint Technician Trainee

*Test Preparation Study Guide
Questions & Answers*

COPYRIGHT NOTICE

This book is SOLELY intended for, is sold ONLY to, and its use is RESTRICTED to individual, bona fide applicants or candidates who qualify by virtue of having seriously filed applications for appropriate license, certificate, professional and/or promotional advancement, higher school matriculation, scholarship, or other legitimate requirements of education and/or governmental authorities.

This book is NOT intended for use, class instruction, tutoring, training, duplication, copying, reprinting, excerption, or adaptation, etc., by:

1) Other publishers
2) Proprietors and/or Instructors of "Coaching" and/or Preparatory Courses
3) Personnel and/or Training Divisions of commercial, industrial, and governmental organizations
4) Schools, colleges, or universities and/or their departments and staffs, including teachers and other personnel
5) Testing Agencies or Bureaus
6) Study groups which seek by the purchase of a single volume to copy and/or duplicate and/or adapt this material for use by the group as a whole without having purchased individual volumes for each of the members of the group
7) Et al.

Such persons would be in violation of appropriate Federal and State statutes.

PROVISION OF LICENSING AGREEMENTS – Recognized educational, commercial, industrial, and governmental institutions and organizations, and others legitimately engaged in educational pursuits, including training, testing, and measurement activities, may address request for a licensing agreement to the copyright owners, who will determine whether, and under what conditions, including fees and charges, the materials in this book may be used them. In other words, a licensing facility exists for the legitimate use of the material in this book on other than an individual basis. However, it is asseverated and affirmed here that the material in this book CANNOT be used without the receipt of the express permission of such a licensing agreement from the Publishers. Inquiries re licensing should be addressed to the company, attention rights and permissions department.

All rights reserved, including the right of reproduction in whole or in part, in any form or by any means, electronic or mechanical, including photocopying, recording, or by any information storage and retrieval system, without permission in writing from the Publisher.

Copyright © 2025 by
National Learning Corporation

212 Michael Drive, Syosset, NY 11791
(516) 921-8888 • www.passbooks.com
E-mail: info@passbooks.com

PASSBOOK® SERIES

THE *PASSBOOK® SERIES* has been created to prepare applicants and candidates for the ultimate academic battlefield – the examination room.

At some time in our lives, each and every one of us may be required to take an examination – for validation, matriculation, admission, qualification, registration, certification, or licensure.

Based on the assumption that every applicant or candidate has met the basic formal educational standards, has taken the required number of courses, and read the necessary texts, the *PASSBOOK® SERIES* furnishes the one special preparation which may assure passing with confidence, instead of failing with insecurity. Examination questions – together with answers – are furnished as the basic vehicle for study so that the mysteries of the examination and its compounding difficulties may be eliminated or diminished by a sure method.

This book is meant to help you pass your examination provided that you qualify and are serious in your objective.

The entire field is reviewed through the huge store of content information which is succinctly presented through a provocative and challenging approach – the question-and-answer method.

A climate of success is established by furnishing the correct answers at the end of each test.

You soon learn to recognize types of questions, forms of questions, and patterns of questioning. You may even begin to anticipate expected outcomes.

You perceive that many questions are repeated or adapted so that you can gain acute insights, which may enable you to score many sure points.

You learn how to confront new questions, or types of questions, and to attack them confidently and work out the correct answers.

You note objectives and emphases, and recognize pitfalls and dangers, so that you may make positive educational adjustments.

Moreover, you are kept fully informed in relation to new concepts, methods, practices, and directions in the field.

You discover that you are actually taking the examination all the time: you are preparing for the examination by "taking" an examination, not by reading extraneous and/or supererogatory textbooks.

In short, this PASSBOOK®, used directedly, should be an important factor in helping you to pass your test.

FINGERPRINT TECHNICIAN TRAINEE

DUTIES

Under close supervision, is trained in and performs beginning-level work in the tasks performed by a fingerprint technician. The work involves the classification and comparison of fingerprint sets and latents to determine positive identification. The employee works under the direct supervision of an administrative superior in the Police Department, learning techniques and procedures on the job. The employee receives permanent appointment as a Fingerprint Technician upon satisfactory completion of one (1) year of continuous service as a permanent competitive Fingerprint Technician Trainee. Performs related work as required.

EXAMPLES OF TYPICAL TASKS

Receives training in, and, under close supervision, assists in performing the following or related tasks: taking fingerprints of persons applying for gun licenses, of candidates for employment and promotion, and of persons requesting good-conduct certificates; classifying fingerprints in accordance with established methods and procedures; searching fingerprint files for the purpose of comparing fingerprints with any prior impressions on records and to disclose criminal records or cases of substitution or impersonation; maintaining fingerprint files and records of pertinent identification data; making regular reports on fingerprints taken, on police records of persons fingerprinted, and on cases of substitution or impersonation.

SCOPE OF THE EXAMINATION

The written test will cover knowledge, skills and/or abilities in such areas as:

1. Pattern recognition, including spatial orientation;
2. Memorization of written and pictorial material;
3. Name and number checking;
4. Understanding and interpreting written material;
5. Preparing written material;
6. Arithmetical reasoning; and
7. Logical reasoning.

HOW TO TAKE A TEST

I. YOU MUST PASS AN EXAMINATION

A. *WHAT EVERY CANDIDATE SHOULD KNOW*

Examination applicants often ask us for help in preparing for the written test. What can I study in advance? What kinds of questions will be asked? How will the test be given? How will the papers be graded?

As an applicant for a civil service examination, you may be wondering about some of these things. Our purpose here is to suggest effective methods of advance study and to describe civil service examinations.

Your chances for success on this examination can be increased if you know how to prepare. Those "pre-examination jitters" can be reduced if you know what to expect. You can even experience an adventure in good citizenship if you know why civil service exams are given.

B. *WHY ARE CIVIL SERVICE EXAMINATIONS GIVEN?*

Civil service examinations are important to you in two ways. As a citizen, you want public jobs filled by employees who know how to do their work. As a job seeker, you want a fair chance to compete for that job on an equal footing with other candidates. The best-known means of accomplishing this two-fold goal is the competitive examination.

Exams are widely publicized throughout the nation. They may be administered for jobs in federal, state, city, municipal, town or village governments or agencies.

Any citizen may apply, with some limitations, such as the age or residence of applicants. Your experience and education may be reviewed to see whether you meet the requirements for the particular examination. When these requirements exist, they are reasonable and applied consistently to all applicants. Thus, a competitive examination may cause you some uneasiness now, but it is your privilege and safeguard.

C. *HOW ARE CIVIL SERVICE EXAMS DEVELOPED?*

Examinations are carefully written by trained technicians who are specialists in the field known as "psychological measurement," in consultation with recognized authorities in the field of work that the test will cover. These experts recommend the subject matter areas or skills to be tested; only those knowledges or skills important to your success on the job are included. The most reliable books and source materials available are used as references. Together, the experts and technicians judge the difficulty level of the questions.

Test technicians know how to phrase questions so that the problem is clearly stated. Their ethics do not permit "trick" or "catch" questions. Questions may have been tried out on sample groups, or subjected to statistical analysis, to determine their usefulness.

Written tests are often used in combination with performance tests, ratings of training and experience, and oral interviews. All of these measures combine to form the best-known means of finding the right person for the right job.

II. HOW TO PASS THE WRITTEN TEST

A. NATURE OF THE EXAMINATION

To prepare intelligently for civil service examinations, you should know how they differ from school examinations you have taken. In school you were assigned certain definite pages to read or subjects to cover. The examination questions were quite detailed and usually emphasized memory. Civil service exams, on the other hand, try to discover your present ability to perform the duties of a position, plus your potentiality to learn these duties. In other words, a civil service exam attempts to predict how successful you will be. Questions cover such a broad area that they cannot be as minute and detailed as school exam questions.

In the public service similar kinds of work, or positions, are grouped together in one "class." This process is known as *position-classification*. All the positions in a class are paid according to the salary range for that class. One class title covers all of these positions, and they are all tested by the same examination.

B. FOUR BASIC STEPS

1) Study the announcement

How, then, can you know what subjects to study? Our best answer is: "Learn as much as possible about the class of positions for which you've applied." The exam will test the knowledge, skills and abilities needed to do the work.

Your most valuable source of information about the position you want is the official exam announcement. This announcement lists the training and experience qualifications. Check these standards and apply only if you come reasonably close to meeting them.

The brief description of the position in the examination announcement offers some clues to the subjects which will be tested. Think about the job itself. Review the duties in your mind. Can you perform them, or are there some in which you are rusty? Fill in the blank spots in your preparation.

Many jurisdictions preview the written test in the exam announcement by including a section called "Knowledge and Abilities Required," "Scope of the Examination," or some similar heading. Here you will find out specifically what fields will be tested.

2) Review your own background

Once you learn in general what the position is all about, and what you need to know to do the work, ask yourself which subjects you already know fairly well and which need improvement. You may wonder whether to concentrate on improving your strong areas or on building some background in your fields of weakness. When the announcement has specified "some knowledge" or "considerable knowledge," or has used adjectives like "beginning principles of..." or "advanced ... methods," you can get a clue as to the number and difficulty of questions to be asked in any given field. More questions, and hence broader coverage, would be included for those subjects which are more important in the work. Now weigh your strengths and weaknesses against the job requirements and prepare accordingly.

3) Determine the level of the position

Another way to tell how intensively you should prepare is to understand the level of the job for which you are applying. Is it the entering level? In other words, is this the position in which beginners in a field of work are hired? Or is it an intermediate or advanced level? Sometimes this is indicated by such words as "Junior" or "Senior" in the class title. Other jurisdictions use Roman numerals to designate the level – Clerk I, Clerk II, for example. The word "Supervisor" sometimes appears in the title. If the level is not indicated by the title, check the description of duties. Will you be working under very close supervision, or will you have responsibility for independent decisions in this work?

4) Choose appropriate study materials

Now that you know the subjects to be examined and the relative amount of each subject to be covered, you can choose suitable study materials. For beginning level jobs, or even advanced ones, if you have a pronounced weakness in some aspect of your training, read a modern, standard textbook in that field. Be sure it is up to date and has general coverage. Such books are normally available at your library, and the librarian will be glad to help you locate one. For entry-level positions, questions of appropriate difficulty are chosen – neither highly advanced questions, nor those too simple. Such questions require careful thought but not advanced training.

If the position for which you are applying is technical or advanced, you will read more advanced, specialized material. If you are already familiar with the basic principles of your field, elementary textbooks would waste your time. Concentrate on advanced textbooks and technical periodicals. Think through the concepts and review difficult problems in your field.

These are all general sources. You can get more ideas on your own initiative, following these leads. For example, training manuals and publications of the government agency which employs workers in your field can be useful, particularly for technical and professional positions. A letter or visit to the government department involved may result in more specific study suggestions, and certainly will provide you with a more definite idea of the exact nature of the position you are seeking.

III. KINDS OF TESTS

Tests are used for purposes other than measuring knowledge and ability to perform specified duties. For some positions, it is equally important to test ability to make adjustments to new situations or to profit from training. In others, basic mental abilities not dependent on information are essential. Questions which test these things may not appear as pertinent to the duties of the position as those which test for knowledge and information. Yet they are often highly important parts of a fair examination. For very general questions, it is almost impossible to help you direct your study efforts. What we can do is to point out some of the more common of these general abilities needed in public service positions and describe some typical questions.

1) General information

Broad, general information has been found useful for predicting job success in some kinds of work. This is tested in a variety of ways, from vocabulary lists to questions about current events. Basic background in some field of work, such as sociology or economics, may be sampled in a group of questions. Often these are principles which have become familiar to most persons through exposure rather than through formal training. It is difficult to advise you how to study for these questions; being alert to the world around you is our best suggestion.

2) Verbal ability

An example of an ability needed in many positions is verbal or language ability. Verbal ability is, in brief, the ability to use and understand words. Vocabulary and grammar tests are typical measures of this ability. Reading comprehension or paragraph interpretation questions are common in many kinds of civil service tests. You are given a paragraph of written material and asked to find its central meaning.

3) Numerical ability

Number skills can be tested by the familiar arithmetic problem, by checking paired lists of numbers to see which are alike and which are different, or by interpreting charts and graphs. In the latter test, a graph may be printed in the test booklet which you are asked to use as the basis for answering questions.

4) Observation

A popular test for law-enforcement positions is the observation test. A picture is shown to you for several minutes, then taken away. Questions about the picture test your ability to observe both details and larger elements.

5) Following directions

In many positions in the public service, the employee must be able to carry out written instructions dependably and accurately. You may be given a chart with several columns, each column listing a variety of information. The questions require you to carry out directions involving the information given in the chart.

6) Skills and aptitudes

Performance tests effectively measure some manual skills and aptitudes. When the skill is one in which you are trained, such as typing or shorthand, you can practice. These tests are often very much like those given in business school or high school courses. For many of the other skills and aptitudes, however, no short-time preparation can be made. Skills and abilities natural to you or that you have developed throughout your lifetime are being tested.

Many of the general questions just described provide all the data needed to answer the questions and ask you to use your reasoning ability to find the answers. Your best preparation for these tests, as well as for tests of facts and ideas, is to be at your physical and mental best. You, no doubt, have your own methods of getting into an exam-taking mood and keeping "in shape." The next section lists some ideas on this subject.

IV. KINDS OF QUESTIONS

Only rarely is the "essay" question, which you answer in narrative form, used in civil service tests. Civil service tests are usually of the short-answer type. Full instructions for answering these questions will be given to you at the examination. But in case this is your first experience with short-answer questions and separate answer sheets, here is what you need to know:

1) Multiple-choice Questions

Most popular of the short-answer questions is the "multiple choice" or "best answer" question. It can be used, for example, to test for factual knowledge, ability to solve problems or judgment in meeting situations found at work.

A multiple-choice question is normally one of three types—
- It can begin with an incomplete statement followed by several possible endings. You are to find the one ending which *best* completes the statement, although some of the others may not be entirely wrong.
- It can also be a complete statement in the form of a question which is answered by choosing one of the statements listed.

- It can be in the form of a problem – again you select the best answer.

Here is an example of a multiple-choice question with a discussion which should give you some clues as to the method for choosing the right answer:

When an employee has a complaint about his assignment, the action which will *best* help him overcome his difficulty is to
    A. discuss his difficulty with his coworkers
    B. take the problem to the head of the organization
    C. take the problem to the person who gave him the assignment
    D. say nothing to anyone about his complaint

In answering this question, you should study each of the choices to find which is best. Consider choice "A" – Certainly an employee may discuss his complaint with fellow employees, but no change or improvement can result, and the complaint remains unresolved. Choice "B" is a poor choice since the head of the organization probably does not know what assignment you have been given, and taking your problem to him is known as "going over the head" of the supervisor. The supervisor, or person who made the assignment, is the person who can clarify it or correct any injustice. Choice "C" is, therefore, correct. To say nothing, as in choice "D," is unwise. Supervisors have and interest in knowing the problems employees are facing, and the employee is seeking a solution to his problem.

2) True/False Questions

The "true/false" or "right/wrong" form of question is sometimes used. Here a complete statement is given. Your job is to decide whether the statement is right or wrong.

SAMPLE: A roaming cell-phone call to a nearby city costs less than a non-roaming call to a distant city.

This statement is wrong, or false, since roaming calls are more expensive.
This is not a complete list of all possible question forms, although most of the others are variations of these common types. You will always get complete directions for answering questions. Be sure you understand *how* to mark your answers – ask questions until you do.

V. RECORDING YOUR ANSWERS

    Computer terminals are used more and more today for many different kinds of exams.
    For an examination with very few applicants, you may be told to record your answers in the test booklet itself. Separate answer sheets are much more common. If this separate answer sheet is to be scored by machine – and this is often the case – it is highly important that you mark your answers correctly in order to get credit.
    An electronic scoring machine is often used in civil service offices because of the speed with which papers can be scored. Machine-scored answer sheets must be marked with a pencil, which will be given to you. This pencil has a high graphite content which responds to the electronic scoring machine. As a matter of fact, stray dots may register as answers, so do not let your pencil rest on the answer sheet while you are pondering the correct answer. Also, if your pencil lead breaks or is otherwise defective, ask for another.

Since the answer sheet will be dropped in a slot in the scoring machine, be careful not to bend the corners or get the paper crumpled.

The answer sheet normally has five vertical columns of numbers, with 30 numbers to a column. These numbers correspond to the question numbers in your test booklet. After each number, going across the page are four or five pairs of dotted lines. These short dotted lines have small letters or numbers above them. The first two pairs may also have a "T" or "F" above the letters. This indicates that the first two pairs only are to be used if the questions are of the true-false type. If the questions are multiple choice, disregard the "T" and "F" and pay attention only to the small letters or numbers.

Answer your questions in the manner of the sample that follows:

32. The largest city in the United States is
    A. Washington, D.C.
    B. New York City
    C. Chicago
    D. Detroit
    E. San Francisco

1) Choose the answer you think is best. (New York City is the largest, so "B" is correct.)
2) Find the row of dotted lines numbered the same as the question you are answering. (Find row number 32)
3) Find the pair of dotted lines corresponding to the answer. (Find the pair of lines under the mark "B.")
4) Make a solid black mark between the dotted lines.

VI. BEFORE THE TEST

Common sense will help you find procedures to follow to get ready for an examination. Too many of us, however, overlook these sensible measures. Indeed, nervousness and fatigue have been found to be the most serious reasons why applicants fail to do their best on civil service tests. Here is a list of reminders:

- Begin your preparation early – Don't wait until the last minute to go scurrying around for books and materials or to find out what the position is all about.
- Prepare continuously – An hour a night for a week is better than an all-night cram session. This has been definitely established. What is more, a night a week for a month will return better dividends than crowding your study into a shorter period of time.
- Locate the place of the exam – You have been sent a notice telling you when and where to report for the examination. If the location is in a different town or otherwise unfamiliar to you, it would be well to inquire the best route and learn something about the building.
- Relax the night before the test – Allow your mind to rest. Do not study at all that night. Plan some mild recreation or diversion; then go to bed early and get a good night's sleep.
- Get up early enough to make a leisurely trip to the place for the test – This way unforeseen events, traffic snarls, unfamiliar buildings, etc. will not upset you.
- Dress comfortably – A written test is not a fashion show. You will be known by number and not by name, so wear something comfortable.

- Leave excess paraphernalia at home – Shopping bags and odd bundles will get in your way. You need bring only the items mentioned in the official notice you received; usually everything you need is provided. Do not bring reference books to the exam. They will only confuse those last minutes and be taken away from you when in the test room.
- Arrive somewhat ahead of time – If because of transportation schedules you must get there very early, bring a newspaper or magazine to take your mind off yourself while waiting.
- Locate the examination room – When you have found the proper room, you will be directed to the seat or part of the room where you will sit. Sometimes you are given a sheet of instructions to read while you are waiting. Do not fill out any forms until you are told to do so; just read them and be prepared.
- Relax and prepare to listen to the instructions
- If you have any physical problem that may keep you from doing your best, be sure to tell the test administrator. If you are sick or in poor health, you really cannot do your best on the exam. You can come back and take the test some other time.

VII. AT THE TEST

The day of the test is here and you have the test booklet in your hand. The temptation to get going is very strong. Caution! There is more to success than knowing the right answers. You must know how to identify your papers and understand variations in the type of short-answer question used in this particular examination. Follow these suggestions for maximum results from your efforts:

1) Cooperate with the monitor

The test administrator has a duty to create a situation in which you can be as much at ease as possible. He will give instructions, tell you when to begin, check to see that you are marking your answer sheet correctly, and so on. He is not there to guard you, although he will see that your competitors do not take unfair advantage. He wants to help you do your best.

2) Listen to all instructions

Don't jump the gun! Wait until you understand all directions. In most civil service tests you get more time than you need to answer the questions. So don't be in a hurry. Read each word of instructions until you clearly understand the meaning. Study the examples, listen to all announcements and follow directions. Ask questions if you do not understand what to do.

3) Identify your papers

Civil service exams are usually identified by number only. You will be assigned a number; you must not put your name on your test papers. Be sure to copy your number correctly. Since more than one exam may be given, copy your exact examination title.

4) Plan your time

Unless you are told that a test is a "speed" or "rate of work" test, speed itself is usually not important. Time enough to answer all the questions will be provided, but this does not mean that you have all day. An overall time limit has been set. Divide the total time (in minutes) by the number of questions to determine the approximate time you have for each question.

5) Do not linger over difficult questions

If you come across a difficult question, mark it with a paper clip (useful to have along) and come back to it when you have been through the booklet. One caution if you do this – be sure to skip a number on your answer sheet as well. Check often to be sure that you have not lost your place and that you are marking in the row numbered the same as the question you are answering.

6) Read the questions

Be sure you know what the question asks! Many capable people are unsuccessful because they failed to *read* the questions correctly.

7) Answer all questions

Unless you have been instructed that a penalty will be deducted for incorrect answers, it is better to guess than to omit a question.

8) Speed tests

It is often better NOT to guess on speed tests. It has been found that on timed tests people are tempted to spend the last few seconds before time is called in marking answers at random – without even reading them – in the hope of picking up a few extra points. To discourage this practice, the instructions may warn you that your score will be "corrected" for guessing. That is, a penalty will be applied. The incorrect answers will be deducted from the correct ones, or some other penalty formula will be used.

9) Review your answers

If you finish before time is called, go back to the questions you guessed or omitted to give them further thought. Review other answers if you have time.

10) Return your test materials

If you are ready to leave before others have finished or time is called, take ALL your materials to the monitor and leave quietly. Never take any test material with you. The monitor can discover whose papers are not complete, and taking a test booklet may be grounds for disqualification.

VIII. EXAMINATION TECHNIQUES

1) Read the general instructions carefully. These are usually printed on the first page of the exam booklet. As a rule, these instructions refer to the timing of the examination; the fact that you should not start work until the signal and must stop work at a signal, etc. If there are any *special* instructions, such as a choice of questions to be answered, make sure that you note this instruction carefully.

2) When you are ready to start work on the examination, that is as soon as the signal has been given, read the instructions to each question booklet, underline any key words or phrases, such as *least, best, outline, describe* and the like. In this way you will tend to answer as requested rather than discover on reviewing your paper that you *listed without describing*, that you selected the *worst* choice rather than the *best* choice, etc.

3) If the examination is of the objective or multiple-choice type – that is, each question will also give a series of possible answers: A, B, C or D, and you are called upon to select the best answer and write the letter next to that answer on your answer paper – it is advisable to start answering each question in turn. There may be anywhere from 50 to 100 such questions in the three or four hours allotted and you can see how much time would be taken if you read through all the questions before beginning to answer any. Furthermore, if you come across a question or group of questions which you know would be difficult to answer, it would undoubtedly affect your handling of all the other questions.

4) If the examination is of the essay type and contains but a few questions, it is a moot point as to whether you should read all the questions before starting to answer any one. Of course, if you are given a choice – say five out of seven and the like – then it is essential to read all the questions so you can eliminate the two that are most difficult. If, however, you are asked to answer all the questions, there may be danger in trying to answer the easiest one first because you may find that you will spend too much time on it. The best technique is to answer the first question, then proceed to the second, etc.

5) Time your answers. Before the exam begins, write down the time it started, then add the time allowed for the examination and write down the time it must be completed, then divide the time available somewhat as follows:
    - If 3-1/2 hours are allowed, that would be 210 minutes. If you have 80 objective-type questions, that would be an average of 2-1/2 minutes per question. Allow yourself no more than 2 minutes per question, or a total of 160 minutes, which will permit about 50 minutes to review.
    - If for the time allotment of 210 minutes there are 7 essay questions to answer, that would average about 30 minutes a question. Give yourself only 25 minutes per question so that you have about 35 minutes to review.

6) The most important instruction is to *read each question* and make sure you know what is wanted. The second most important instruction is to *time yourself properly* so that you answer every question. The third most important instruction is to *answer every question*. Guess if you have to but include something for each question. Remember that you will receive no credit for a blank and will probably receive some credit if you write something in answer to an essay question. If you guess a letter – say "B" for a multiple-choice question – you may have guessed right. If you leave a blank as an answer to a multiple-choice question, the examiners may respect your feelings but it will not add a point to your score. Some exams may penalize you for wrong answers, so in such cases *only*, you may not want to guess unless you have some basis for your answer.

7) Suggestions
    a. Objective-type questions
        1. Examine the question booklet for proper sequence of pages and questions
        2. Read all instructions carefully
        3. Skip any question which seems too difficult; return to it after all other questions have been answered
        4. Apportion your time properly; do not spend too much time on any single question or group of questions

5. Note and underline key words – *all, most, fewest, least, best, worst, same, opposite,* etc.
6. Pay particular attention to negatives
7. Note unusual option, e.g., unduly long, short, complex, different or similar in content to the body of the question
8. Observe the use of "hedging" words – *probably, may, most likely,* etc.
9. Make sure that your answer is put next to the same number as the question
10. Do not second-guess unless you have good reason to believe the second answer is definitely more correct
11. Cross out original answer if you decide another answer is more accurate; do not erase until you are ready to hand your paper in
12. Answer all questions; guess unless instructed otherwise
13. Leave time for review

  b. Essay questions
    1. Read each question carefully
    2. Determine exactly what is wanted. Underline key words or phrases.
    3. Decide on outline or paragraph answer
    4. Include many different points and elements unless asked to develop any one or two points or elements
    5. Show impartiality by giving pros and cons unless directed to select one side only
    6. Make and write down any assumptions you find necessary to answer the questions
    7. Watch your English, grammar, punctuation and choice of words
    8. Time your answers; don't crowd material

8) Answering the essay question

Most essay questions can be answered by framing the specific response around several key words or ideas. Here are a few such key words or ideas:

M's: manpower, materials, methods, money, management
P's: purpose, program, policy, plan, procedure, practice, problems, pitfalls, personnel, public relations

  a. Six basic steps in handling problems:
    1. Preliminary plan and background development
    2. Collect information, data and facts
    3. Analyze and interpret information, data and facts
    4. Analyze and develop solutions as well as make recommendations
    5. Prepare report and sell recommendations
    6. Install recommendations and follow up effectiveness

  b. Pitfalls to avoid
    1. *Taking things for granted* – A statement of the situation does not necessarily imply that each of the elements is necessarily true; for example, a complaint may be invalid and biased so that all that can be taken for granted is that a complaint has been registered

2. *Considering only one side of a situation* – Wherever possible, indicate several alternatives and then point out the reasons you selected the best one
3. *Failing to indicate follow up* – Whenever your answer indicates action on your part, make certain that you will take proper follow-up action to see how successful your recommendations, procedures or actions turn out to be
4. *Taking too long in answering any single question* – Remember to time your answers properly

IX. AFTER THE TEST

Scoring procedures differ in detail among civil service jurisdictions although the general principles are the same. Whether the papers are hand-scored or graded by machine we have described, they are nearly always graded by number. That is, the person who marks the paper knows only the number – never the name – of the applicant. Not until all the papers have been graded will they be matched with names. If other tests, such as training and experience or oral interview ratings have been given, scores will be combined. Different parts of the examination usually have different weights. For example, the written test might count 60 percent of the final grade, and a rating of training and experience 40 percent. In many jurisdictions, veterans will have a certain number of points added to their grades.

After the final grade has been determined, the names are placed in grade order and an eligible list is established. There are various methods for resolving ties between those who get the same final grade – probably the most common is to place first the name of the person whose application was received first. Job offers are made from the eligible list in the order the names appear on it. You will be notified of your grade and your rank as soon as all these computations have been made. This will be done as rapidly as possible.

People who are found to meet the requirements in the announcement are called "eligibles." Their names are put on a list of eligible candidates. An eligible's chances of getting a job depend on how high he stands on this list and how fast agencies are filling jobs from the list.

When a job is to be filled from a list of eligibles, the agency asks for the names of people on the list of eligibles for that job. When the civil service commission receives this request, it sends to the agency the names of the three people highest on this list. Or, if the job to be filled has specialized requirements, the office sends the agency the names of the top three persons who meet these requirements from the general list.

The appointing officer makes a choice from among the three people whose names were sent to him. If the selected person accepts the appointment, the names of the others are put back on the list to be considered for future openings.

That is the rule in hiring from all kinds of eligible lists, whether they are for typist, carpenter, chemist, or something else. For every vacancy, the appointing officer has his choice of any one of the top three eligibles on the list. This explains why the person whose name is on top of the list sometimes does not get an appointment when some of the persons lower on the list do. If the appointing officer chooses the second or third eligible, the No. 1 eligible does not get a job at once, but stays on the list until he is appointed or the list is terminated.

X. HOW TO PASS THE INTERVIEW TEST

The examination for which you applied requires an oral interview test. You have already taken the written test and you are now being called for the interview test – the final part of the formal examination.

You may think that it is not possible to prepare for an interview test and that there are no procedures to follow during an interview. Our purpose is to point out some things you can do in advance that will help you and some good rules to follow and pitfalls to avoid while you are being interviewed.

What is an interview supposed to test?

The written examination is designed to test the technical knowledge and competence of the candidate; the oral is designed to evaluate intangible qualities, not readily measured otherwise, and to establish a list showing the relative fitness of each candidate – as measured against his competitors – for the position sought. Scoring is not on the basis of "right" and "wrong," but on a sliding scale of values ranging from "not passable" to "outstanding." As a matter of fact, it is possible to achieve a relatively low score without a single "incorrect" answer because of evident weakness in the qualities being measured.

Occasionally, an examination may consist entirely of an oral test – either an individual or a group oral. In such cases, information is sought concerning the technical knowledges and abilities of the candidate, since there has been no written examination for this purpose. More commonly, however, an oral test is used to supplement a written examination.

Who conducts interviews?

The composition of oral boards varies among different jurisdictions. In nearly all, a representative of the personnel department serves as chairman. One of the members of the board may be a representative of the department in which the candidate would work. In some cases, "outside experts" are used, and, frequently, a businessman or some other representative of the general public is asked to serve. Labor and management or other special groups may be represented. The aim is to secure the services of experts in the appropriate field.

However the board is composed, it is a good idea (and not at all improper or unethical) to ascertain in advance of the interview who the members are and what groups they represent. When you are introduced to them, you will have some idea of their backgrounds and interests, and at least you will not stutter and stammer over their names.

What should be done before the interview?

While knowledge about the board members is useful and takes some of the surprise element out of the interview, there is other preparation which is more substantive. It *is* possible to prepare for an oral interview – in several ways:

1) Keep a copy of your application and review it carefully before the interview

This may be the only document before the oral board, and the starting point of the interview. Know what education and experience you have listed there, and the sequence and dates of all of it. Sometimes the board will ask you to review the highlights of your experience for them; you should not have to hem and haw doing it.

2) Study the class specification and the examination announcement

Usually, the oral board has one or both of these to guide them. The qualities, characteristics or knowledges required by the position sought are stated in these documents. They offer valuable clues as to the nature of the oral interview. For example, if the job involves supervisory responsibilities, the announcement will usually indicate that knowledge of modern supervisory methods and the qualifications of the candidate as a supervisor will be tested. If so, you can expect such questions, frequently in the form of a hypothetical situation which you are expected to solve. NEVER go into an oral without knowledge of the duties and responsibilities of the job you seek.

3) Think through each qualification required

Try to visualize the kind of questions you would ask if you were a board member. How well could you answer them? Try especially to appraise your own knowledge and background in each area, *measured against the job sought*, and identify any areas in which you are weak. Be critical and realistic – do not flatter yourself.

4) Do some general reading in areas in which you feel you may be weak

For example, if the job involves supervision and your past experience has NOT, some general reading in supervisory methods and practices, particularly in the field of human relations, might be useful. Do NOT study agency procedures or detailed manuals. The oral board will be testing your understanding and capacity, not your memory.

5) Get a good night's sleep and watch your general health and mental attitude

You will want a clear head at the interview. Take care of a cold or any other minor ailment, and of course, no hangovers.

What should be done on the day of the interview?

Now comes the day of the interview itself. Give yourself plenty of time to get there. Plan to arrive somewhat ahead of the scheduled time, particularly if your appointment is in the fore part of the day. If a previous candidate fails to appear, the board might be ready for you a bit early. By early afternoon an oral board is almost invariably behind schedule if there are many candidates, and you may have to wait. Take along a book or magazine to read, or your application to review, but leave any extraneous material in the waiting room when you go in for your interview. In any event, relax and compose yourself.

The matter of dress is important. The board is forming impressions about you – from your experience, your manners, your attitude, and your appearance. Give your personal appearance careful attention. Dress your best, but not your flashiest. Choose conservative, appropriate clothing, and be sure it is immaculate. This is a business interview, and your appearance should indicate that you regard it as such. Besides, being well groomed and properly dressed will help boost your confidence.

Sooner or later, someone will call your name and escort you into the interview room. *This is it.* From here on you are on your own. It is too late for any more preparation. But remember, you asked for this opportunity to prove your fitness, and you are here because your request was granted.

What happens when you go in?

The usual sequence of events will be as follows: The clerk (who is often the board stenographer) will introduce you to the chairman of the oral board, who will introduce you to the other members of the board. Acknowledge the introductions before you sit down. Do not be surprised if you find a microphone facing you or a stenotypist sitting by. Oral interviews are usually recorded in the event of an appeal or other review.

Usually the chairman of the board will open the interview by reviewing the highlights of your education and work experience from your application – primarily for the benefit of the other members of the board, as well as to get the material into the record. Do not interrupt or comment unless there is an error or significant misinterpretation; if that is the case, do not hesitate. But do not quibble about insignificant matters. Also, he will usually ask you some question about your education, experience or your present job – partly to get you to start talking and to establish the interviewing "rapport." He may start the actual questioning, or turn it over to one of the other members. Frequently, each member undertakes the questioning on a particular area, one in which he is perhaps most competent, so you can expect each member to participate in the examination. Because time is limited, you may also expect some rather abrupt switches in the direction the questioning takes, so do not be upset by it. Normally, a board member will not pursue a single line of questioning unless he discovers a particular strength or weakness.

After each member has participated, the chairman will usually ask whether any member has any further questions, then will ask you if you have anything you wish to add. Unless you are expecting this question, it may floor you. Worse, it may start you off on an extended, extemporaneous speech. The board is not usually seeking more information. The question is principally to offer you a last opportunity to present further qualifications or to indicate that you have nothing to add. So, if you feel that a significant qualification or characteristic has been overlooked, it is proper to point it out in a sentence or so. Do not compliment the board on the thoroughness of their examination – they have been sketchy, and you know it. If you wish, merely say, "No thank you, I have nothing further to add." This is a point where you can "talk yourself out" of a good impression or fail to present an important bit of information. Remember, *you close the interview yourself*.

The chairman will then say, "That is all, Mr. _____, thank you." Do not be startled; the interview is over, and quicker than you think. Thank him, gather your belongings and take your leave. Save your sigh of relief for the other side of the door.

How to put your best foot forward

Throughout this entire process, you may feel that the board individually and collectively is trying to pierce your defenses, seek out your hidden weaknesses and embarrass and confuse you. Actually, this is not true. They are obliged to make an appraisal of your qualifications for the job you are seeking, and they want to see you in your best light. Remember, they must interview all candidates and a non-cooperative candidate may become a failure in spite of their best efforts to bring out his qualifications. Here are 15 suggestions that will help you:

1) Be natural – Keep your attitude confident, not cocky

If you are not confident that you can do the job, do not expect the board to be. Do not apologize for your weaknesses, try to bring out your strong points. The board is interested in a positive, not negative, presentation. Cockiness will antagonize any board member and make him wonder if you are covering up a weakness by a false show of strength.

2) Get comfortable, but don't lounge or sprawl

Sit erectly but not stiffly. A careless posture may lead the board to conclude that you are careless in other things, or at least that you are not impressed by the importance of the occasion. Either conclusion is natural, even if incorrect. Do not fuss with your clothing, a pencil or an ashtray. Your hands may occasionally be useful to emphasize a point; do not let them become a point of distraction.

3) Do not wisecrack or make small talk

This is a serious situation, and your attitude should show that you consider it as such. Further, the time of the board is limited – they do not want to waste it, and neither should you.

4) Do not exaggerate your experience or abilities
In the first place, from information in the application or other interviews and sources, the board may know more about you than you think. Secondly, you probably will not get away with it. An experienced board is rather adept at spotting such a situation, so do not take the chance.

5) If you know a board member, do not make a point of it, yet do not hide it
Certainly you are not fooling him, and probably not the other members of the board. Do not try to take advantage of your acquaintanceship – it will probably do you little good.

6) Do not dominate the interview
Let the board do that. They will give you the clues – do not assume that you have to do all the talking. Realize that the board has a number of questions to ask you, and do not try to take up all the interview time by showing off your extensive knowledge of the answer to the first one.

7) Be attentive
You only have 20 minutes or so, and you should keep your attention at its sharpest throughout. When a member is addressing a problem or question to you, give him your undivided attention. Address your reply principally to him, but do not exclude the other board members.

8) Do not interrupt
A board member may be stating a problem for you to analyze. He will ask you a question when the time comes. Let him state the problem, and wait for the question.

9) Make sure you understand the question
Do not try to answer until you are sure what the question is. If it is not clear, restate it in your own words or ask the board member to clarify it for you. However, do not haggle about minor elements.

10) Reply promptly but not hastily
A common entry on oral board rating sheets is "candidate responded readily," or "candidate hesitated in replies." Respond as promptly and quickly as you can, but do not jump to a hasty, ill-considered answer.

11) Do not be peremptory in your answers
A brief answer is proper – but do not fire your answer back. That is a losing game from your point of view. The board member can probably ask questions much faster than you can answer them.

12) Do not try to create the answer you think the board member wants
He is interested in what kind of mind you have and how it works – not in playing games. Furthermore, he can usually spot this practice and will actually grade you down on it.

13) Do not switch sides in your reply merely to agree with a board member
Frequently, a member will take a contrary position merely to draw you out and to see if you are willing and able to defend your point of view. Do not start a debate, yet do not surrender a good position. If a position is worth taking, it is worth defending.

14) Do not be afraid to admit an error in judgment if you are shown to be wrong
The board knows that you are forced to reply without any opportunity for careful consideration. Your answer may be demonstrably wrong. If so, admit it and get on with the interview.

15) Do not dwell at length on your present job
The opening question may relate to your present assignment. Answer the question but do not go into an extended discussion. You are being examined for a *new* job, not your present one. As a matter of fact, try to phrase ALL your answers in terms of the job for which you are being examined.

Basis of Rating
Probably you will forget most of these "do's" and "don'ts" when you walk into the oral interview room. Even remembering them all will not ensure you a passing grade. Perhaps you did not have the qualifications in the first place. But remembering them will help you to put your best foot forward, without treading on the toes of the board members.

Rumor and popular opinion to the contrary notwithstanding, an oral board wants you to make the best appearance possible. They know you are under pressure – but they also want to see how you respond to it as a guide to what your reaction would be under the pressures of the job you seek. They will be influenced by the degree of poise you display, the personal traits you show and the manner in which you respond.

ABOUT THIS BOOK

This book contains tests divided into Examination Sections. Go through each test, answering every question in the margin. We have also attached a sample answer sheet at the back of the book that can be removed and used. At the end of each test look at the answer key and check your answers. On the ones you got wrong, look at the right answer choice and learn. Do not fill in the answers first. Do not memorize the questions and answers, but understand the answer and principles involved. On your test, the questions will likely be different from the samples. Questions are changed and new ones added. If you understand these past questions you should have success with any changes that arise. Tests may consist of several types of questions. We have additional books on each subject should more study be advisable or necessary for you. Finally, the more you study, the better prepared you will be. This book is intended to be the last thing you study before you walk into the examination room. Prior study of relevant texts is also recommended. NLC publishes some of these in our Fundamental Series. Knowledge and good sense are important factors in passing your exam. Good luck also helps. So now study this Passbook, absorb the material contained within and take that knowledge into the examination. Then do your best to pass that exam.

EXAMINATION SECTION

EXAMINATION SECTION
TEST 1

DIRECTIONS: Each question or incomplete statement is followed by several suggested answers or completions. Select the one that BEST answers the question or completes the statement. *PRINT THE LETTER OF THE CORRECT ANSWER IN THE SPACE AT THE RIGHT.*

1. You and a co-worker have been given a rush job to classify 50 sets of fingerprints. Although you started out with 25 sets each, the ones you were given were less complicated; and when you are finished, your co-worker still has several sets to work on. It would be BEST for you to

   A. go back to your normal assignment
   B. offer to help your co-worker with the work he has left
   C. recheck the work you have done since you have extra time
   D. wait until your co-worker is finished before turning in your work, so it doesn't look as though he was *goofing off*

   1.____

2. Several prospective police department employees arrive to be fingerprinted. One of the people arrives a few minutes later than the others but insists he must be fingerprinted first since he has important personal business to attend to. In addition, he is insolent and impolite. It would be BEST for you to

   A. fingerprint this person first so he will stop bothering you
   B. politely explain to this person that he must wait his turn
   C. refuse to fingerprint the person until he apologizes to you
   D. write a memo to the personnel office stating that you think this person should not be hired

   2.____

3. While you are filing a fingerprint card, you notice another card that is misfiled. It would be BEST for you to

   A. ask your co-workers why the card is in the wrong place
   B. leave the card where it is since someone may have a good reason for putting it there
   C. remove the card from the drawer and refile it in the correct place
   D. send the card to your supervisor with a note explaining that you found it misfiled

   3.____

4. You receive a telephone call from someone claiming to be a police officer who asks you for information about the criminal record of another person. This information might be in the files you have access to. The BEST thing for you to do would be to

   A. ask him to write you a letter requesting the information
   B. check the files and give him the information if you have it
   C. explain to him that such requests must be made through the office handling such records
   D. tell him you do not have the information

   4.____

5. Assume your supervisor gives you a group of fingerprinting cards to file. In glancing over them, you notice they have not been classified as most cards are before they are filed. The BEST thing you can do in this situation is

   5.____

1

A. ask a technician to classify the fingerprints and then file them
B. file the cards anyway, since that is what you were told to do
C. leave the cards on your desk until your supervisor asks you whether you filed them; then explain why you did not do so
D. point out the omission to your supervisor before you file the cards

6. You are filing a large stack of fingerprint cards when a newly hired probationary patrolman arrives at your office to be fingerprinted before starting work. For you to finish your filing before fingerprinting him would be

    A. *correct;* if you stop in the middle of your filing, you may make mistakes when you return to it
    B. *incorrect;* the patrolman might overhear confidential information while waiting for you
    C. *correct;* you should not start to fingerprint someone until you can devote your full attention to the job
    D. *incorrect;* it is not good practice to keep someone waiting while you do paperwork which could be done later

7. Your supervisor gives you a rush job alphabetizing a stack of fingerprint cards. You start the job, but are distracted by a conversation with a fellow employee and forget to finish the work. When your supervisor asks you for the completed work, the BEST thing for you to tell him would be that you

    A. did not understand his instructions
    B. forgot to finish the job but will do it as soon as you can
    C. have been working steadily on the job but have not had time to finish it
    D. were given a more important assignment

8. Your office has only one telephone line which is sometimes used to call a technician or trainee for rush work. You must make a lengthy personal telephone call during working hours. For you to make the call on the office telephone would be

    A. *proper;* employees must occasionally handle personal matters during working hours
    B. *improper;* a rush call could be delayed while you have the phone tied up
    C. *proper;* you should not leave the office to make personal calls during working hours
    D. *improper;* other people in the office might overhear your personal business

9. While using the fingerprint files, you find a card for one of your neighbors. The card indicates that many years earlier the person was convicted of attempted murder, though your neighbor has told you he was arrested for the crime but never convicted. The BEST thing for you to do would be to

    A. accuse your neighbor of lying to you about his past
    B. change the card so that it indicates arrest without conviction
    C. say nothing to anyone about this police record
    D. tell your neighbor the police have an incorrect record for him

10. You have been instructed that a technician or trainee must be available in the fingerprint unit for rush work. On a certain day your co-workers are out of the office at lunch time. The BEST thing for you to do would be to

A. ask a clerk from another office to cover your office while you go out to lunch
B. lock the office and take your lunch hour
C. put off your lunch hour until a technician or trainee returns
D. take a quick break for lunch and handle any rush work when you return

11. If a secretary who has never worked in the fingerprint unit returns some fingerprint cards that his supervisor has borrowed, the BEST way to have the cards refiled accurately would be to

    A. explain the filing system to him so that he can re-file them himself
    B. have him refile them and check his work later
    C. refile them yourself when you have a chance
    D. tell him his supervisor is responsible for refiling borrowed cards

11.____

12. After you have been working for a short time, you think you have developed a system which will make the filing of fingerprint cards more efficient. The BEST thing for you to do would be to

    A. ask your co-workers to try the new method for a few days to see if it really works
    B. describe the new method to your supervisor and ask her if she thinks it would help
    C. say nothing about your idea since it has probably been tried unsuccessfully by someone else
    D. use the new method yourself but say nothing to anyone else since they might resent your interference

12.____

13. The MOST appropriate statement for Mr. Jones to make when answering the telephone in his office is:

    A. Fingerprint Unit, Mr. Jones speaking
    B. Good morning, Fingerprint Unit
    C. Hello, who is this?
    D. May I help you?

13.____

14. The work space used by any clerk should be well organized. In order to work efficiently, it is MOST important that the worker's desk be arranged so that

    A. materials needed for work are within easy reach
    B. personal belongings do not take up any drawer space
    C. it is neat in appearance
    D. the top of the desk is clear of all papers

14.____

15. When you arrive at work one day, you find a note from your supervisor with instructions for a special assignment she wants you to perform. However, you do not understand certain of the instructions. It would be BEST for you to

    A. carry out the instructions the way you think they should be done
    B. find your supervisor and ask her to clarify the instructions
    C. show the note to your co-workers and ask them what they think you should do
    D. tell your supervisor, when she asks you for the completed assignment, that you have not done the work because you did not understand the instructions

15.____

16. In most offices some workers gossip about other people there. With regard to such gossip, a new employee in the fingerprint unit should

16.____

A. be interested in any information he can learn about his co-workers
B. discuss the information with the supervisor in order to learn the truth
C. pass the information on to those workers who would be interested in the news
D. try to ignore the information since there is usually little truth to it

17. Closing file drawers immediately after use is important MAINLY because it

    A. is a safety precaution
    B. is otherwise possible to file material in the wrong file drawer
    C. makes it possible for other workers to use adjoining file drawers
    D. protects the tabs on the file folders from ripping

18. The FIRST step in filing cards alphabetically is to

    A. count the cards
    B. divide the cards into groups of ten
    C. inspect each card to insure that it is filled out completely
    D. rearrange the cards in alphabetical order

19. If you cannot find the folder on Michael Hillston in an alphabetic file, you should

    A. assume that the folder is lost
    B. check other places where the folder could easily have been misfiled, like Hilston and Hillson
    C. look through all of the alphabetic files to see whether the folder was misplaced
    D. return to your other work and check for the folder again the next day

20. Of the following, the type of filing system used in the MOST efficiently run office depends MOSTLY on the

    A. way records are used or requested
    B. geographical location of the office
    C. skill of clerical personnel who do the filing
    D. number of filing clerks employed

21. The MOST important reason for well-organized files is to insure that

    A. business papers and records can easily be found
    B. company documents will be arranged alphabetically
    C. file space will be efficiently utilized for business purposes
    D. it is possible to identify the individual who committed any errors

Questions 22-26.

DIRECTIONS: Questions 22 through 26 are to be answered based on an alphabetical arrangement of the following list of names.

Walker, Carol J.	Wacht, Michael	Wade, Ethel
Wall, Fredrick	Wall, Francis	Wall, Frank
Wachs, Paul	Walker, Carol L.	Wagner, Arthur
Walters, Daniel	Wade, Ellen	Wald, William
Wagner, Allen	Walters, David	Walker, Carmen

22. The 4th name on the alphabetized list would be 22._____
    A. Wade, Ellen   B. Wade, Ethel
    C. Wagner, Allen   D. Wagner, Arthur

23. The 7th name on the alphabetized list would be 23._____
    A. Walker, Carmen   B. Walker, Carol J.
    C. Walker, Carol L.   D. Wald, William

24. The name that would come immediately AFTER Wagner, Arthur on the alphabetized list would be 24._____
    A. Wade, Ethel   B. Wagner, Allen
    C. Wald, William   D. Walker, Carol L.

25. The name that would come immediately BEFORE Wall, Frank would be 25._____
    A. Wall, Francis   B. Wall, Fredrick
    C. Walters, David   D. Walters, Daniel

26. The 12th name on the alphabetized list would be 26._____
    A. Walker, Carol L.   B. Wald, William
    C. Wall, Francis   D. Wall, Frank

Questions 27-35.

DIRECTIONS: Questions 27 through 35 are to be answered SOLELY on the basis of the following information and the following list of individuals and identification numbers.

Assume that the police department is planning to conduct a statistical study of individuals who have been convicted of crimes during a certain year. For the purpose of this study, identification numbers are being assigned to individuals in the following manner:

The first two digits indicate the age of the individual. The third digit indicates the sex of the individual:
  1. male
  2. female
The fourth digit indicates the type of crime involved:
  1. criminal homicide
  2. forcible rape
  3. robbery
  4. aggravated assault
  5. burglary
  6. larceny
  7. auto theft
  8. other

The fifth and sixth digits indicate the month in which the conviction occurred:
  01. January
  02. February, etc.

| Abbott, Richard | 271304 | Morris, Chris | 212705 |
| Collins, Terry | 352111 | Owens, William | 231412 |

Elders, Edward	191207	Parker, Leonard	291807
George, Linda	182809	Robinson, Charles	311102
Hill Leslie	251702	Sands, Jean	202610
Jones, Jackie	301106	Smith, Michael	421308
Lewis, Edith	402406	Turner, Donald	191601
Mack, Helen	332509	White, Barbara	242803

27. The number of women on the above list is 27.___

    A. 6   B. 7   C. 8   D. 9

28. The two convictions which occurred during February were for the crimes of 28.___

    A. aggravated assault and auto theft
    B. auto theft and criminal homicide
    C. burglary and larceny
    D. forcible rape and robbery

29. The ONLY man convicted of auto theft was 29.___

    A. Richard Abbott   B. Leslie Hill
    C. Chris Morris   D. Leonard Parker

30. The number of people on the list who were 25 years old or older is 30.___

    A. 6   B. 7   C. 8   D. 9

31. The OLDEST person on the list is 31.___

    A. Terry Collins   B. Edith Lewis
    C. Helen Mack   D. Michael Smith

32. The two people on the list who are the same age are 32.___

    A. Richard Abbott and Michael Smith
    B. Edward Elders and Donald Turner
    C. Linda George and Helen Mack
    D. Leslie Hill and Charles Robinson

33. A 28-year-old man who was convicted of aggravated assault in October would have identification number 33.___

    A. 281410   B. 281509   C. 282311   D. 282409

34. A 33-year-old woman convicted in April of criminal homicide would have identification number 34.___

    A. 331140   B. 331204   C. 332014   D. 332104

35. The number of people on the above list who were convicted during the first six months of the year is 35.___

    A. 6   B. 7   C. 8   D. 9

Questions 36-45.

DIRECTIONS: Questions 36 through 45 test how good you are at catching mistakes in typing or printing. In each question, the name and address in Column II should be an exact copy of the name and address in Column I. Mark your answer:
    A. if there is no mistake in either name or address
    B. if there are mistakes in both name and address
    C. if there is a mistake only in the name
    D. if there is a mistake only in the address.

	COLUMN I	COLUMN II	
36.	Arturo Rodriguez 2156 Cruger Avenue Bronx, New York 10446	Arturo Rodrigues 2156 Cruger Avenue Bronx, New York 10446	36._____
37.	Helen McCabe 2044 East 19 Street Brooklyn, New York 11204	Helen McCabe 2040 East 19 Street Brooklyn, New York 11204	37._____
38.	Charles Martin 526 West 160 Street New York, N.Y. 10022	Charles Martin 526 West 160 Street New York, N.Y. 10022	38._____
39.	Morris Rabinowitz 31 Avenue M Brooklyn, N.Y. 11216	Morris Rabinowitz 31 Avenue N Brooklyn, N.Y. 11216	39._____
40.	Joseph DiSilva 63-84 Saunders Road Rego Park, N.Y. 11431	Joseph Disilva 64-83 Saunders Road Rego Park, N.Y. 11431	40._____
41.	Linda Polansky 2225 Fenton Avenue Bronx, N.Y. 10464	Linda Polansky 2255 Fenton Avenue Bronx, N.Y. 10464	41._____
42.	Alfred Klein 260 Hillside Terrace Staten Island, N.Y. 15545	Alfred Klein 260 Hillside Terrace Staten Island, N.Y. 15545	42._____
43.	William McDonnell 504 E. 55 Street New York, N.Y. 10103	William McConnell 504 E. 55 Street New York, N.Y. 10108	43._____
44.	Angela Cipolla 41-11 Parsons Avenue Flushing, N.Y. 11446	Angela Cipola 41-11 Parsons Avenue Flushing, N.Y. 11446	44._____
45.	Julie Sheridan 1212 Ocean Avenue Brooklyn, N.Y. 11237	Julia Sheridan 1212 Ocean Avenue Brooklyn, N.Y. 11237	45._____

KEY (CORRECT ANSWERS)

1. B	11. C	21. A	31. D	41. D
2. B	12. B	22. B	32. B	42. A
3. C	13. A	23. D	33. A	43. B
4. C	14. A	24. C	34. D	44. C
5. D	15. B	25. A	35. C	45. C
6. D	16. D	26. D	36. C	
7. B	17. A	27. B	37. D	
8. B	18. D	28. B	38. A	
9. C	19. B	29. B	39. D	
10. C	20. A	30. D	40. B	

TEST 2

DIRECTIONS: Each question or incomplete statement is followed by several suggested answers or completions. Select the one that BEST answers the question or completes the statement. *PRINT THE LETTER OF THE CORRECT ANSWER IN THE SPACE AT THE RIGHT.*

Questions 1-10.

DIRECTIONS: Questions 1 through 10 are to be answered ONLY on the basis of the following information.
Column I consists of identification numbers of fingerprints.
Column II shows different ways of arranging the corresponding identification numbers.

The identification numbers of the fingerprints in Column I begin and end with a capital letter and have an eight-digit number in between. The identification numbers in Column I are to be arranged according to the following rules:

1. In alphabetical order according to the first letter.
2. When two or more identification numbers have the same first letter, in alphabetical order according to the last letter.
3. When two or more identification numbers have the same first AND last letters, in numerical order, beginning with the lowest number.

The identification numbers in Column I are numbered 1 through 5. In Column II, the numbers 1 through 5 are arranged in four different ways to show different arrangements of the corresponding identification numbers. Choose the answer in Column II in which the identification numbers are arranged according to the above rules.

SAMPLE QUESTION

COLUMN I
(1) E75044127B
(2) B96399104A
(3) B93939086A
(4) B47064465H
(5) B99040922A

COLUMN II
A. 4, 1, 3, 2, 5
B. 4, 1, 2, 3, 5
C. 4, 3, 2, 5, 1
D. 3, 2, 5, 4, 1

In the sample question, the four identification numbers starting with B should be put before the identification number starting with E. The identification numbers starting with B and ending with A should be put before the identification number starting with B and ending with M. The three identification numbers starting with B and ending with A should be listed in numerical order, beginning with the lowest number. The CORRECT way to arrange the identification numbers, therefore, is:

(3) B93939086A
(2) B96399104A
(5) B99040922A
(4) B47064465H
(1) E75044127B

Since the order of arrangement is 3, 2, 5, 4, 1, the answer to the sample question is D.

COLUMN I

1. (1) B33886897B
   (2) B38386882B
   (3) D33389862B
   (4) D33336887D
   (5) B38888697D

2. (1) E11664554M
   (2) F11164544M
   (3) F11614455N
   (4) E11665454M
   (5) F16161545N

3. (1) C86611355W
   (2) C68631533V
   (3) G88633331W
   (4) C68833515V
   (5) G68833511W

4. (1) R73665312J
   (2) P73685512J
   (3) P73968511J
   (4) R73665321K
   (5) R63985211K

5. (1) X33661222U
   (2) Y83961323V
   (3) Y88991123V
   (4) X33691233U
   (5) X38691333U

6. (1) B22838847W
   (2) B28833874V
   (3) B22288344X
   (4) B28238374V
   (5) B28883347V

7. (1) H44477447G
   (2) H47444777G
   (3) H74777477C
   (4) H44747447G
   (5) H77747447C

8. (1) G11143447G
   (2) G15133388C
   (3) C15134378G
   (4) G11534477C
   (5) C15533337C

COLUMN II

A. 5, 1, 3, 4, 2
B. 1, 2, 5, 3, 4
C. 1, 2, 5, 4, 3
D. 2, 1, 4, 5, 3

A. 4, 1, 2, 5, 3
B. 2, 4, 1, 5, 3
C. 4, 2, 1, 3, 5
D. 1, 4, 2, 3, 5

A. 2, 4, 1, 5, 3
B. 1, 2, 4, 3, 5
C. 1, 2, 5, 4, 3
D. 1, 2, 4, 3, 5

A. 3, 2, 1, 4, 5
B. 2, 3, 5, 1, 4
C. 2, 3, 1, 5, 4
D. 3, 1, 5, 2, 4

A. 1, 4, 5, 2, 3
B. 4, 5, 1, 3, 2
C. 4, 5, 1, 2, 3
D. 4, 1, 5, 2, 3

A. 4, 5, 2, 3, 1
B. 4, 2, 5, 1, 3
C. 4, 5, 2, 1, 3
D. 4, 1, 5, 2, 3

A. 1, 3, 5, 4, 2
B. 3, 1, 5, 2, 4
C. 1, 4, 2, 3, 5
D. 3, 5, 1, 4, 2

A. 3, 5, 1, 4, 2
B. 1, 4, 3, 2, 5
C. 5, 3, 4, 2, 1
D. 4, 3, 1, 2, 5

1.___
2.___
3.___
4.___
5.___
6.___
7.___
8.___

9. (1) J96693369F
    (2) J66939339F
    (3) J96693693E
    (4) J96663933E
    (5) J69639363F

    A. 4, 3, 2, 5, 1
    B. 2, 5, 4, 1, 3
    C. 2, 5, 4, 3, 1
    D. 3, 4, 5, 2, 1

    9.____

10. (1) L15567834Z
    (2) P11587638Z
    (3) M51567688Z
    (4) O55578784Z
    (5) N53588783Z

    A. 3, 1, 5, 2, 4
    B. 1, 3, 5, 4, 2
    C. 1, 3, 5, 2, 4
    D. 3, 1, 5, 4, 2

    10.____

Questions 11-17.

DIRECTIONS: Each of Questions 11 through 17 consists of a long series of letters and numbers under Column I and four short series of letters and numbers under Column II. For each question, choose the short series of letters and numbers which is entirely and exactly the same as some part of the long series.

SAMPLE QUESTION

COLUMN I
JG13572XY89WB14

COLUMN II
A. 1372Y8
B. XYWB14
C. 72XY89
D. J13572

In each of choices A, B, and D, one or more of the letters and numbers in the series in Column I is omitted. Only option C reproduces a segment of the series entirely and exactly. Therefore, C is the CORRECT answer to the sample question.

COLUMN I

11. P473R365M442V5W

COLUMN II
A. P47365
B. 73P365
C. 365M44
D. 5X42V5

11.____

12. 865CG441V21SS59

A. 1V12SS
B. V21SS5
C. 5GC441
D. 894CG4

12.____

13. 1E227FE383L4700

A. E27FE3
B. EF838L
C. EL4700
D. 83L470

13.____

14. 77J646G54NPB318

A. NPB318
B. J646J5
C. 4G54NP
D. C54NPB

14.____

15. 85887T358W24A93
    A. 858887
    B. W24A93
    C. 858W24
    D. 87T353

16. E104RY796B33H14
    A. 04RY79
    B. E14RYR
    C. 96B3H1
    D. RY7996

17. W58NP12141DE07M
    A. 8MP121
    B. W53NP1
    C. 14DE07
    D. 12141D

Questions 18-27

DIRECTIONS: Questions 18 through 27 are to be answered on the basis of the following information.

The phonetic filing system is a method of filing names in which the alphabet is reduced to key code letters. The six key letters and their equivalents are as follows:

KEY LETTERS	EQUIVALENTS
b	p, f, v
c	s, k, g, j, q, x, z
d	t
l	none
m	n
r	none

A key letter represents itself.
Vowels (a, e, i, o, and u) and the letters w, h, and y are omitted.
For example, the name GILMAN would be represented as follows:

G is represented by the key letter c
I is a vowel and is omitted
L is a key letter and represents itself
M is a key letter and represents itself
A is a vowel and is omitted
N is represented by the key letter M

Therefore, the phonetic filing code for the name GILMAN is CLMM.

18. The phonetic filing code for the name FITZGERALD would be
    A. BDCCRLD   B. BDCRLD   C. BDZCRLD   D. BTZCRLD

19. The phonetic filing code CLBR may represent any one of the following names EXCEPT
    A. Calprey   B. Flower   C. Glover   D. Silver

5 (#2)

20. The phonetic filing code LDM may represent any one of the following names EXCEPT   20.____
    A. Halden   B. Hilton   C. Walton   D. Wilson

21. The phonetic filing code for the name RODRIGUEZ would be   21.____
    A. RDRC   B. RDRCC   C. RDRCZ   D. RTRCC

22. The phonetic filing code for the name MAXWELL would be   22.____
    A. MCLL   B. MCWL   C. MCWLL   D. MXLL

23. The phonetic filing code for the name ANDERSON would be   23.____
    A. AMDRCM   B. ENDRSM   C. MDRCM   D. NDERCN

24. The phonetic filing code for the name SAVITSKY would be   24.____
    A. CBDCC   B. CBDCY   C. SBDCC   D. SVDCC

25. The phonetic filing code CMC may represent any one of the following names EXCEPT   25.____
    A. James   B. Jayes   C. Johns   D. Jones

26. The ONLY one of the following names that could be represented by the phonetic filing code CDDDM would be   26.____
    A. Catalano   B. Chesterton
    C. Cittadino   D. Cuttlerman

27. The ONLY one of the following names that could be represented by the phonetic filing code LLMCM would be   27.____
    A. Ellington   B. Hallerman
    C. Inslerman   D. Willingham

Questions 28-35.

DIRECTIONS: Questions 28 through 35 test how well you compare figures. Each question shows figures that have a certain feature in common. Mark the letter of the choice that also has that feature.

28.   28.____

29.

30.

31.

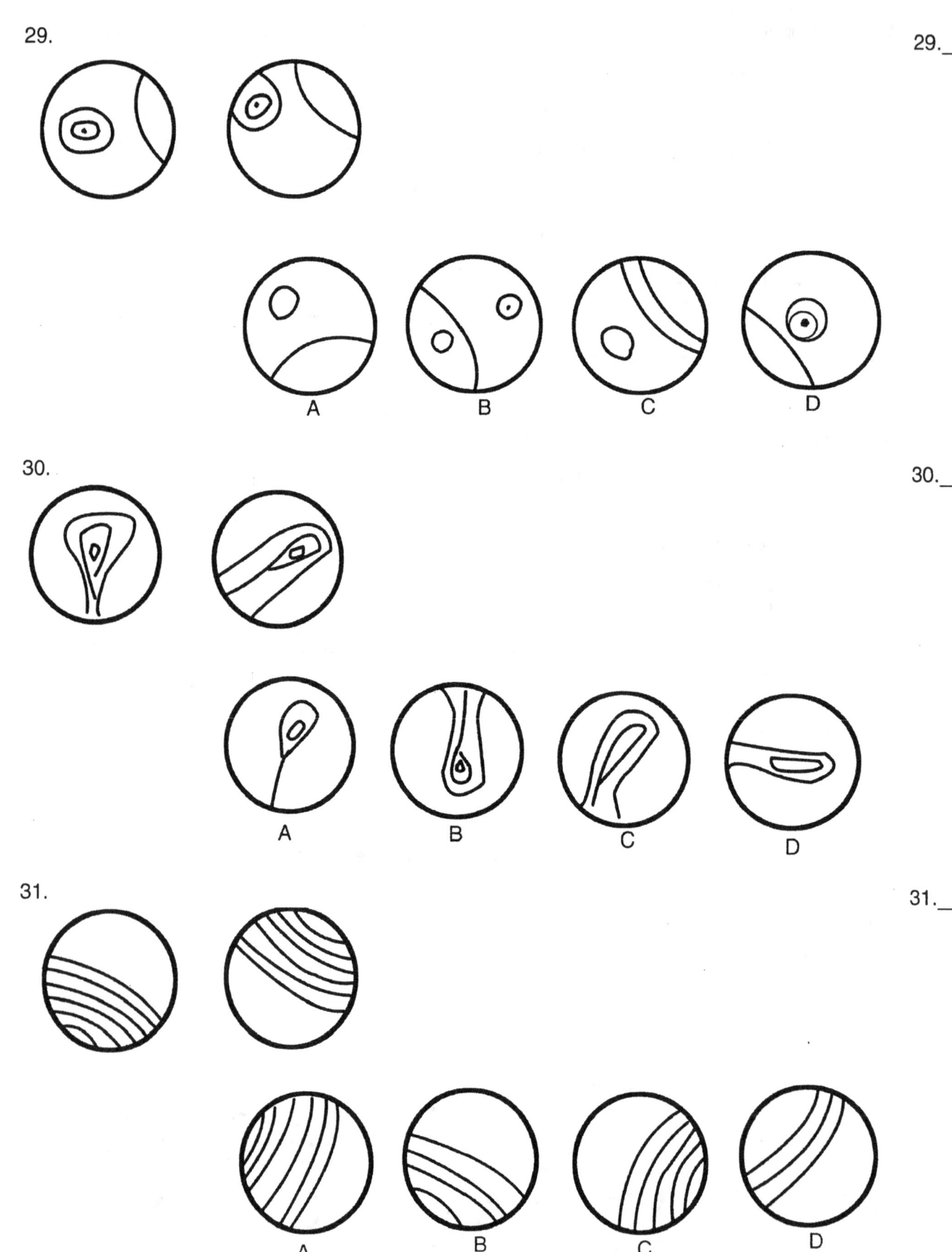

32.

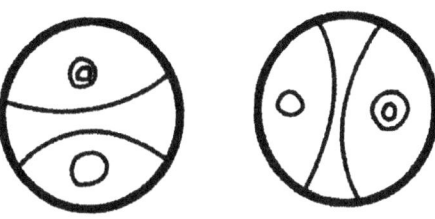

 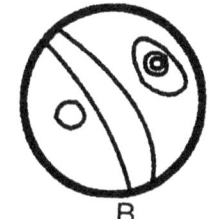 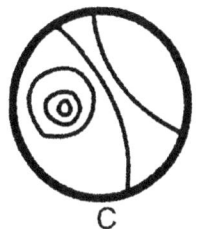 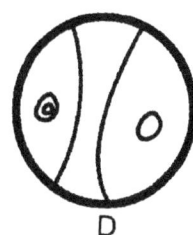
A B C D

33.

 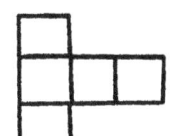

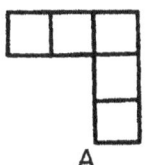 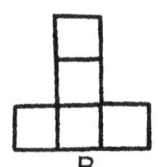 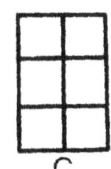 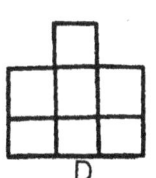
A B C D

34.

 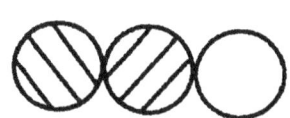

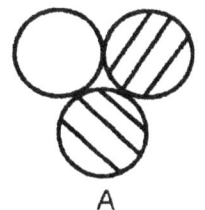 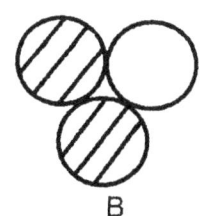 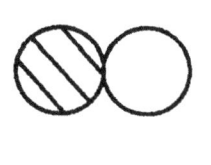 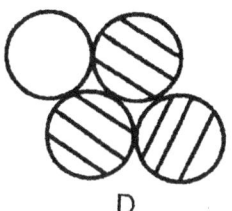
A B C D

35. 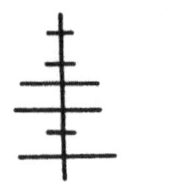 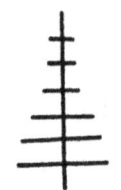 35.___

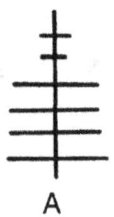   
A　　　　B　　　　C　　　　D

KEY (CORRECT ANSWERS)

1.	B	16.	A
2.	D	17.	D
3.	A	18.	A
4.	C	19.	B
5.	A	20.	D
6.	B	21.	B
7.	D	22.	A
8.	C	23.	C
9.	A	24.	A
10.	B	25.	B
11.	C	26.	C
12.	B	27.	D
13.	D	28.	C
14.	A	29.	D
15.	B	30.	B

31. A
32. D
33. B
34. A
35. D

FINGERPRINT SCIENCE
EXAMINATION SECTION

DIRECTIONS FOR THIS SECTION:
For each of questions 1 through 20, choose the one of the four fingerprints lettered A, B, C, or D that is identical to the single fingerprint near the question number. *PRINT THE LETTER OF THE CORRECT ANSWER IN THE SPACE AT THE RIGHT.*

TEST 1

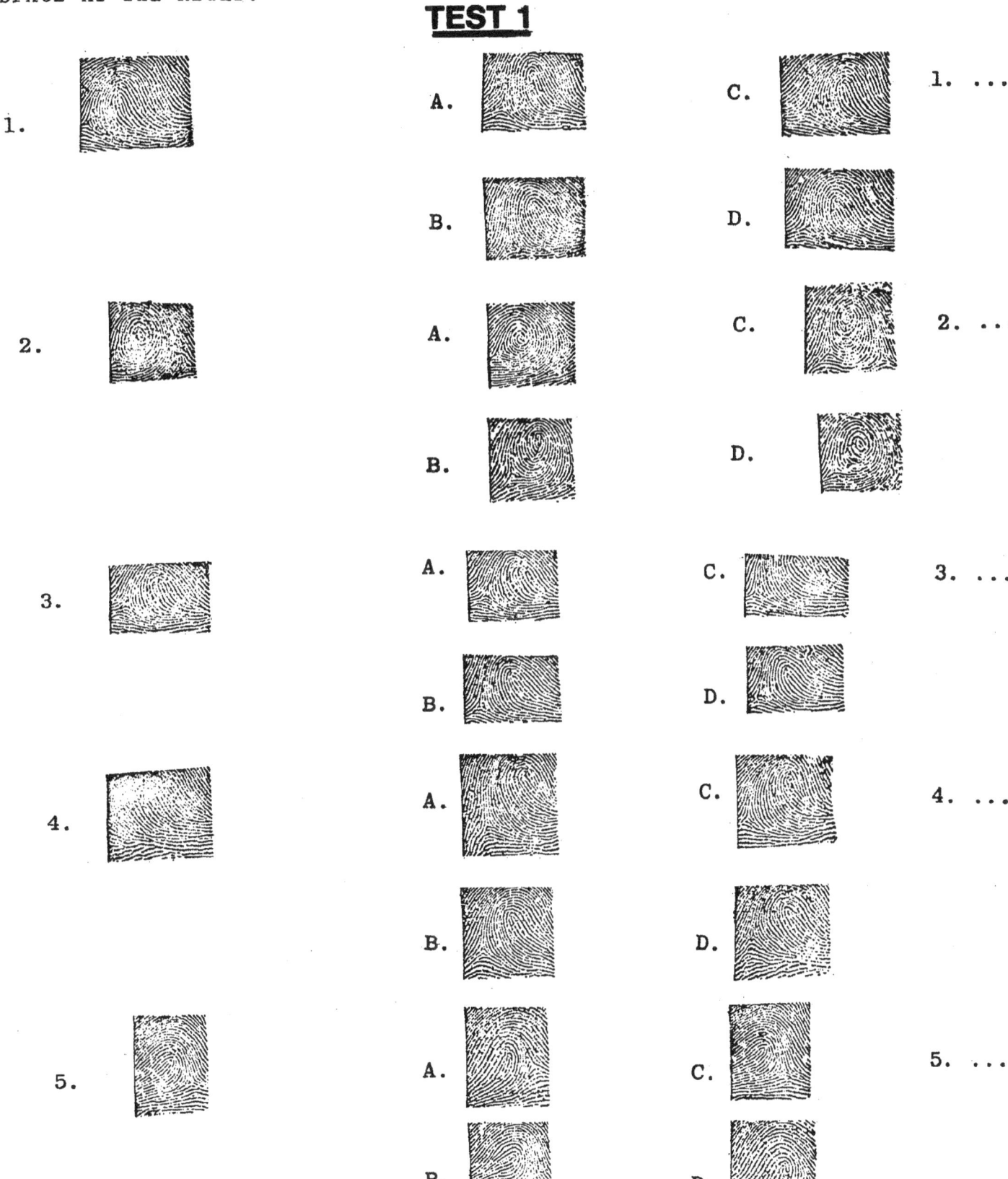

Test 1

6.   A.   C.   6. ...
     B.   D.

7.   A.   C.   7. ...
     B.   D.

8.   A.   C.   8. ...
     B.   D.

9.   A.   C.   9. ...
     B.   D.

10. A.   C.   10. ...
     B.   D.

Test 1

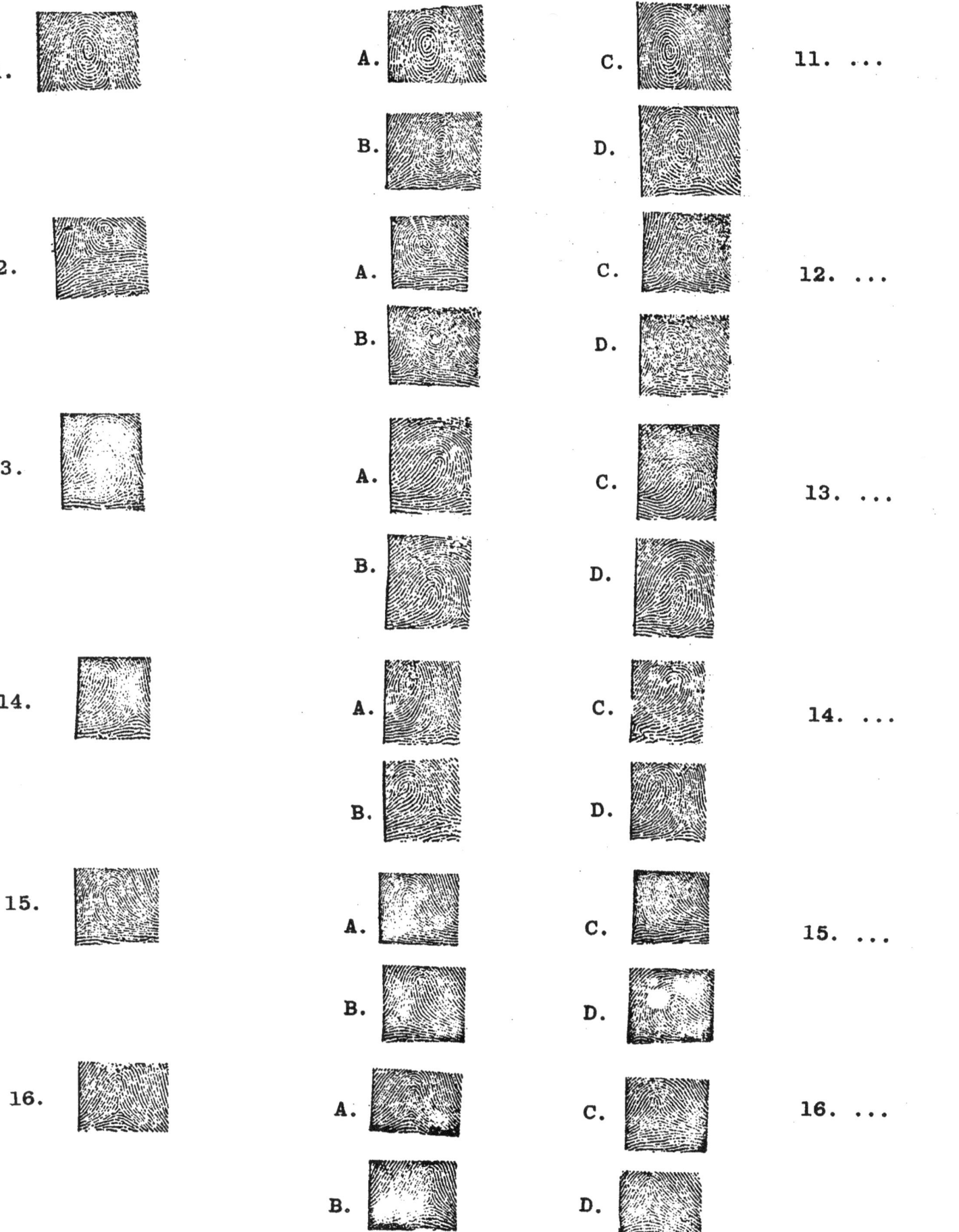

Test 1

17.   A.   C.   17. ....
       B.   D.

18.   A.   C.   18. ....
       B.   D.

19.   A.   C.   19. ....
       B.   D.

20.   A.   C.   20. ....
       B.   D.

Test 2

DIRECTIONS FOR THIS SECTION:
Questions 1 through 20 are based on the group of fingerprints lettered A through Z below.
For questions 1 through 20, choose from this group of fingerprints the fingerprint that is identical to the one in each question.
Print the *letter* of the correct answer next to each *numbered* question.

TEST 2

Test 2/KEYS

___ 1.   ___ 6.   ___ 11.   ___ 16.

___ 2.   ___ 7.   ___ 12.   ___ 17.

___ 3.   ___ 8.   ___ 13.   ___ 18.

___ 4.   ___ 9.   ___ 14.   ___ 19.

___ 5.   ___ 10. ___ 15.   ___ 20.

KEYS (CORRECT ANSWERS)

TEST 1				TEST 2			
1.	C	11.	C	1.	R	11.	V
2.	D	12.	A	2.	Z	12.	X
3.	A	13.	D	3.	I	13.	B
4.	D	14.	D	4.	G	14.	P
5.	C	15.	A	5.	F	15.	M
6.	C	16.	B	6.	O	16.	E
7.	D	17.	A	7.	D	17.	C
8.	C	18.	D	8.	U	18.	N
9.	C	19.	A	9.	L	19.	K
10.	B	20.	B	10.	H	20.	S

ABSTRACT REASONING

COMMENTARY

Since intelligence exists in many forms or phases and the theory of differential aptitudes is now firmly established in testing, other manifestations and measurements of intelligence than verbal or purely arithmetical must be identified and measured.

Classification inventory, or figure classification, involves the aptitude of form perception, i.e., the ability to perceive pertinent detail in objects or in pictorial or graphic material. It involves making visual comparisons and discriminations and discerning slight differences in shapes and shading figures and widths and lengths of lines.

Leading examples of presentation are the figure analogy and the figure classification. The section that follows presents progressive and varied samplings of this type of question.

SAMPLE QUESTIONS

DIRECTIONS: In each of these sample questions, look at the symbols in the first two boxes. Something about the three symbols in the first box makes them alike; something about the two symbols in the other box with the question mark makes them alike. Look for some characteristic that is common to all symbols in the same box, yet makes them different from the symbols in the other box. Among the five answer choices, find the symbol that can BEST be substituted for the question mark, because it is *like* the symbols in the second box, and, for the same reason, different from those in the first box.

1.

In sample question 1, all the symbols in the first box are vertical lines. The second box has two lines, one broken and one solid. Their *likeness* to each other consists in their being horizontal; and their being horizontal makes them *different* from the vertical lines in the other box. The answer must be the only one of the five lettered choices that is a horizontal line, ether broken or solid. Therefore, the CORRECT answer is C.

2.

The CORRECT answer is A.

EXAMINATION SECTION

TEST 1

DIRECTIONS: In each of these questions, look at the symbols in the first two boxes. Something about the three symbols in the first box makes them alike; something about the two symbols in the other box with the question mark makes them alike. Look for some characteristic that is common to all symbols in the same box, yet makes them different from the symbols in the other box. Among the five answer choices, find the symbol that can BEST be substituted for the question mark, because it is *like* the symbols in the second box, and, for the same reason, different from those in the first box. PRINT THE LETTER OF THE CORRECT ANSWER IN THE SPACE AT THE RIGHT.

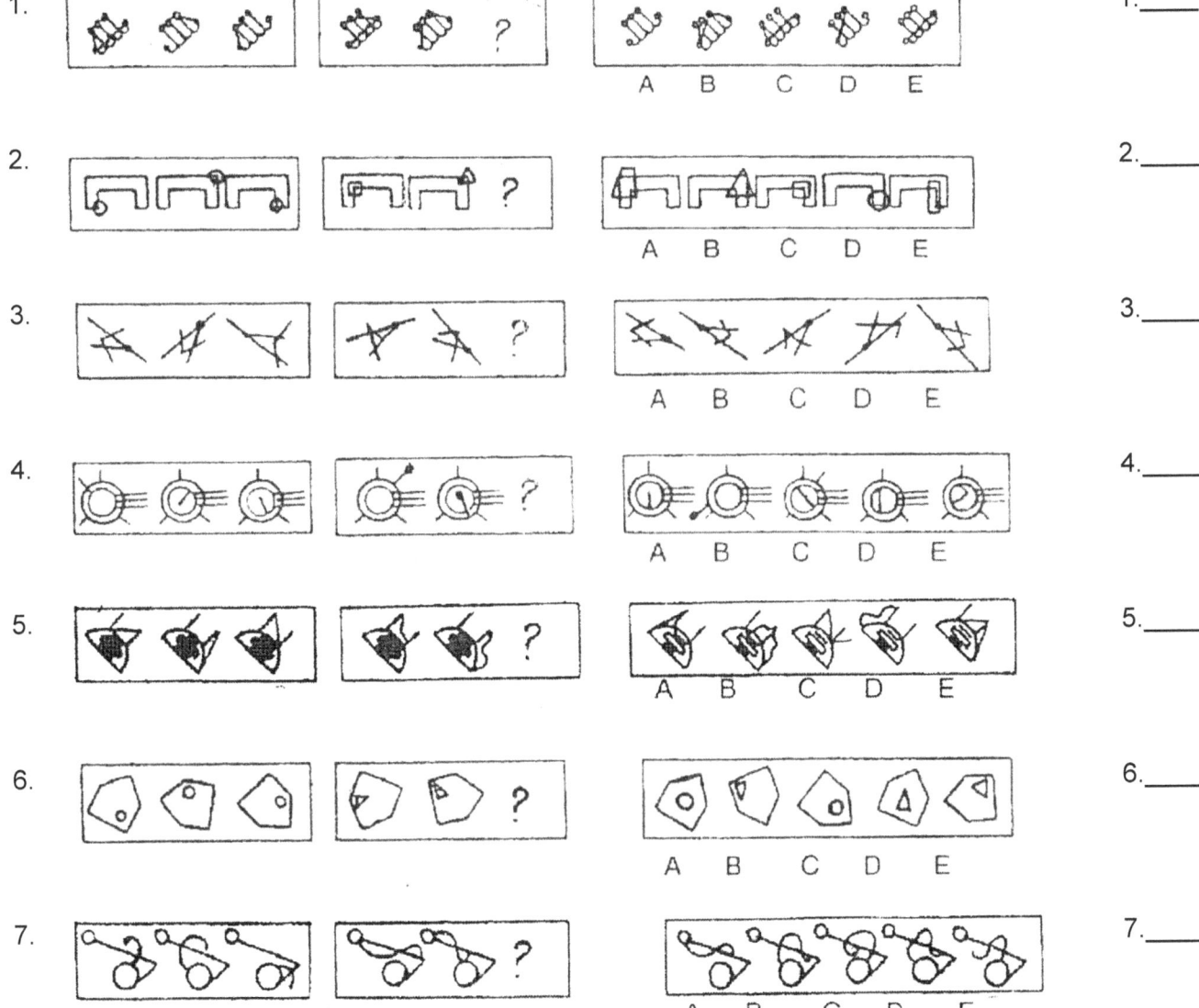

2 (#1)

8.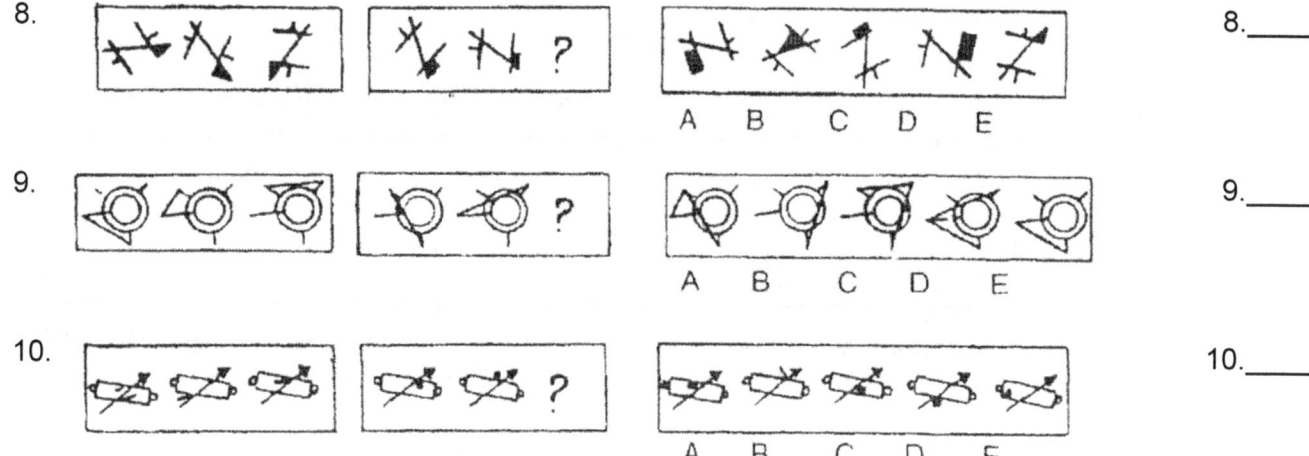

9.

10.

KEY (CORRECT ANSWERS)

1.	B	6.	B
2.	C	7.	A
3.	C	8.	C
4.	B	9.	B
5.	D	10.	D

TEST 2

DIRECTIONS: In each of these questions, look at the symbols in the first two boxes. Something about the three symbols in the first box makes them alike; something about the two symbols in the other box with the question mark makes them alike. Look for some characteristic that is common to all symbols in the same box, yet makes them different from the symbols in the other box. Among the five answer choices, find the symbol that can BEST be substituted for the question mark, because it is *like* the symbols in the second box, and, for the same reason, different from those in the first box. *PRINT THE LETTER OF THE CORRECT ANSWER IN THE SPACE AT THE RIGHT.*

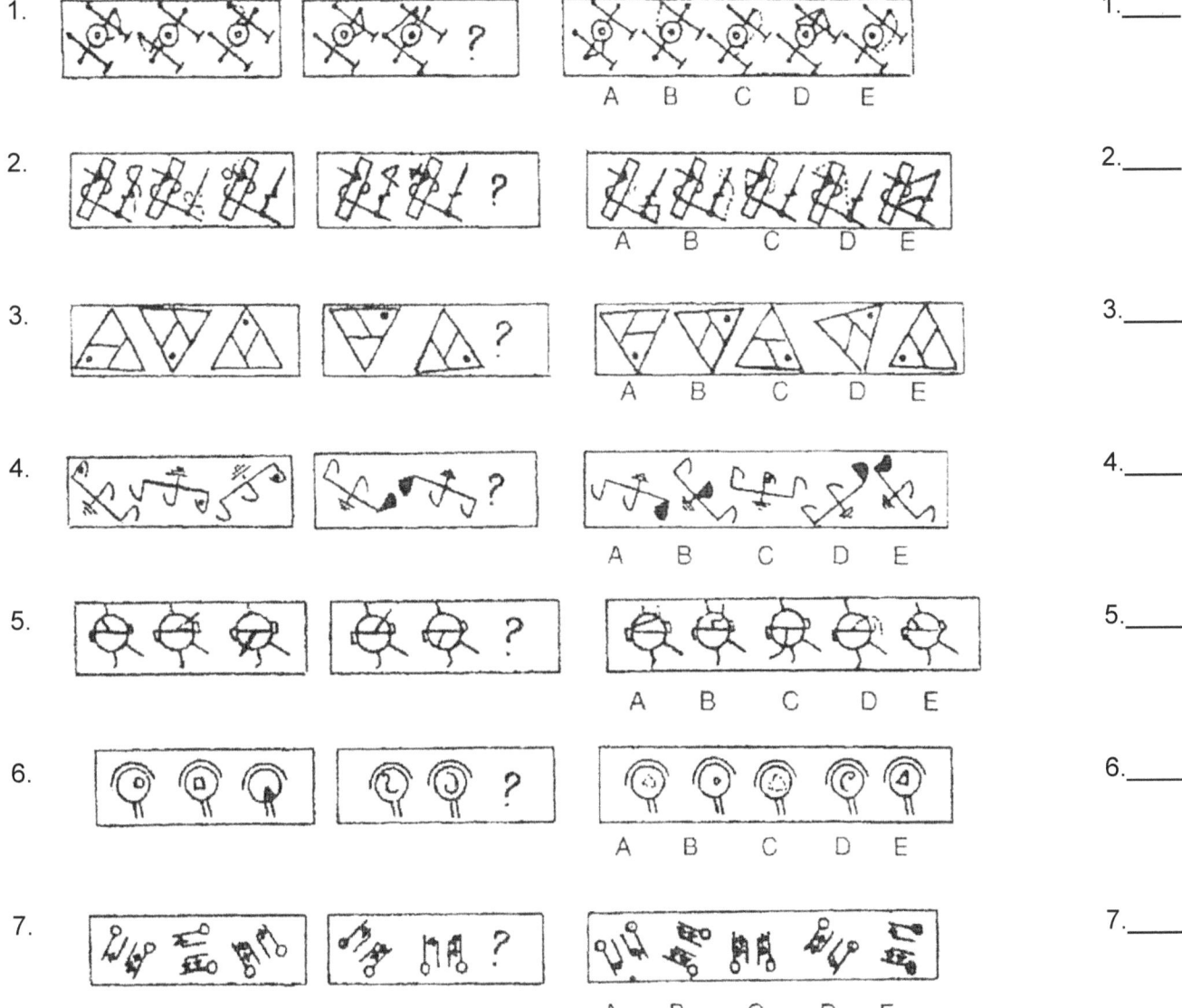

2 (#2)

8.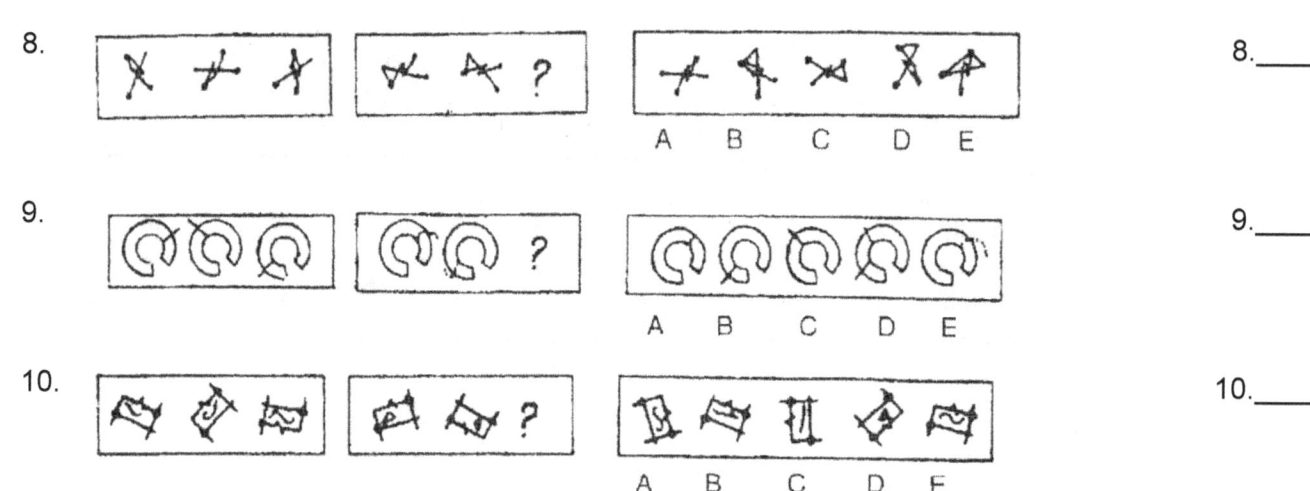

9.

10.

KEY (CORRECT ANSWERS)

1.	A	6.	D
2.	A	7.	D
3.	A	8.	C
4.	D	9.	E
5.	E	10.	D

TEST 3

DIRECTIONS: In each of these questions, look at the symbols in the first two boxes. Something about the three symbols in the first box makes them alike; something about the two symbols in the other box with the question mark makes them alike. Look for some characteristic that is common to all symbols in the same box, yet makes them different from the symbols in the other box. Among the five answer choices, find the symbol that can BEST be substituted for the question mark, because it is *like* the symbols in the second box, and, for the same reason, different from those in the first box. *PRINT THE LETTER OF THE CORRECT ANSWER IN THE SPACE AT THE RIGHT.*

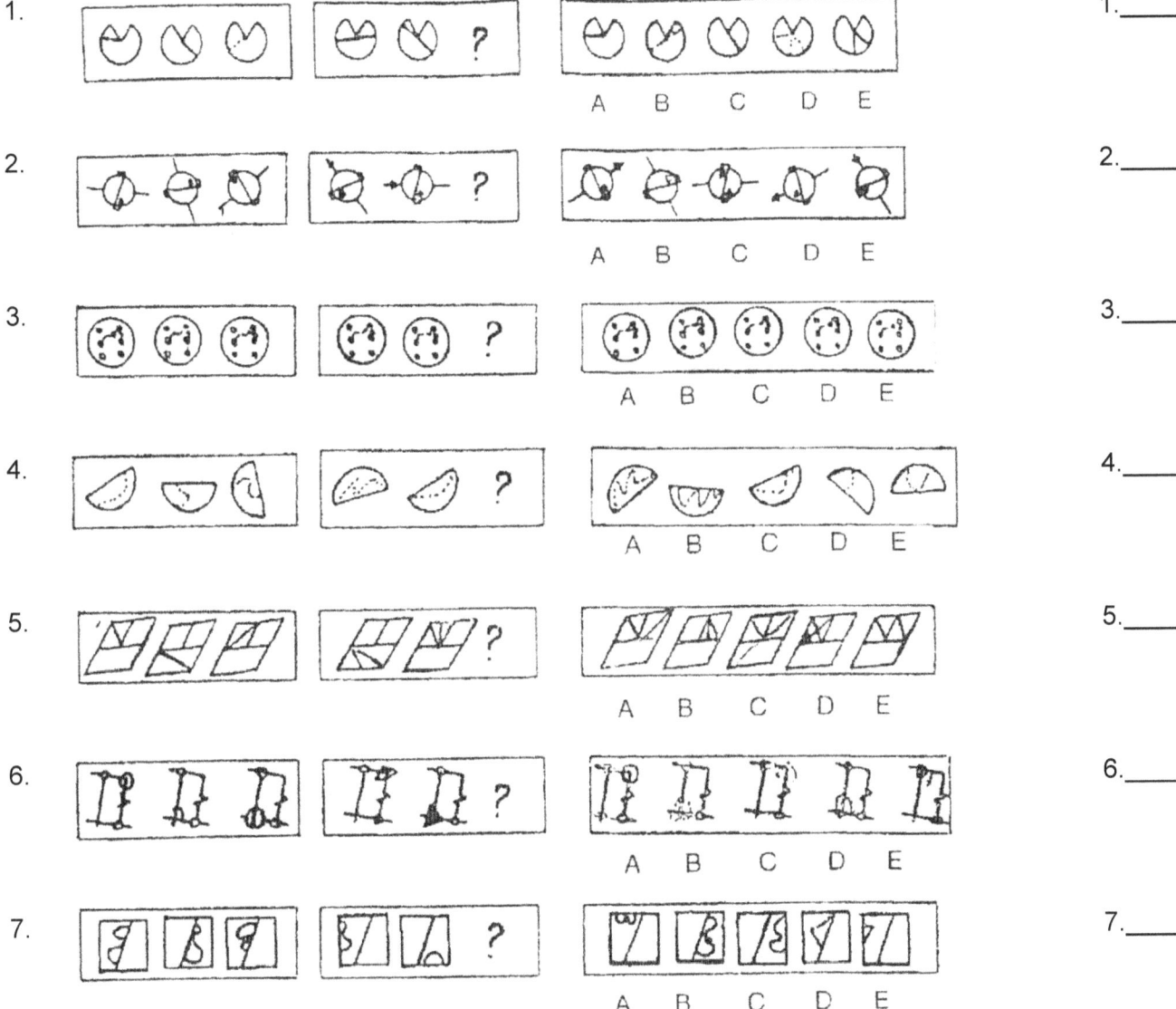

2 (#3)

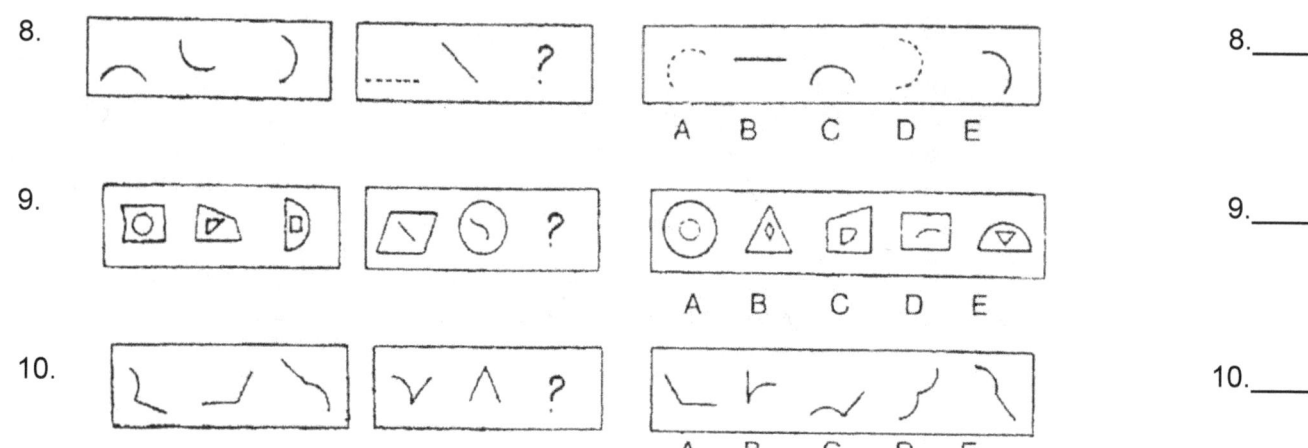

KEY (CORRECT ANSWERS)

1.	B	6.	C
2.	E	7.	C
3.	C	8.	B
4.	A	9.	D
5.	B	10.	B

PROBLEM SENSITIVITY

This section of the exam measures your ability to choose the course of action that should be taken first in critical situations.

Sample Questions

1. What should an officer do first when investigating an incident?

    A. Write a report of the incident.
    B. Inform other police officers of the incident.
    C. Proceed to the scene of the incident.
    D. Interview witnesses.

Getting the correct information to the emergency medical personnel is extremely important. It is suggested that you, the police officer, make the call if possible, or assign the task to a person who appears calm. If you are alone at the accident scene, do not leave the victim until breathing is restored, all bleeding has been stopped, the victim is no longer in danger of further injury, and all precautions have been taken against shock. When the emergency medical personnel arrive, brief them as to what happened to the victim, the type of first aid you have administered, and the physical status of the victim.

2. When the emergency medical personnel arrives at the accident scene, you first should tell them:

    A. how long the victim's breathing has been restored.
    B. how long the bleeding has been stopped.
    C. that the victim appeared to be going into shock.
    D. the type of first aid you administered.

KEY (CORRECT ANSWERS)

1. C
2. D

IDENTIFYING THEMES AND IDEAS

One section of the exam will test your ability to determine or understand a theme or idea presented in pictures or in written passages.

Sample Question

The three pictures shown below contain a common idea or theme. From the four concepts listed in question 1, choose the one concept that is common to all of the pictures.

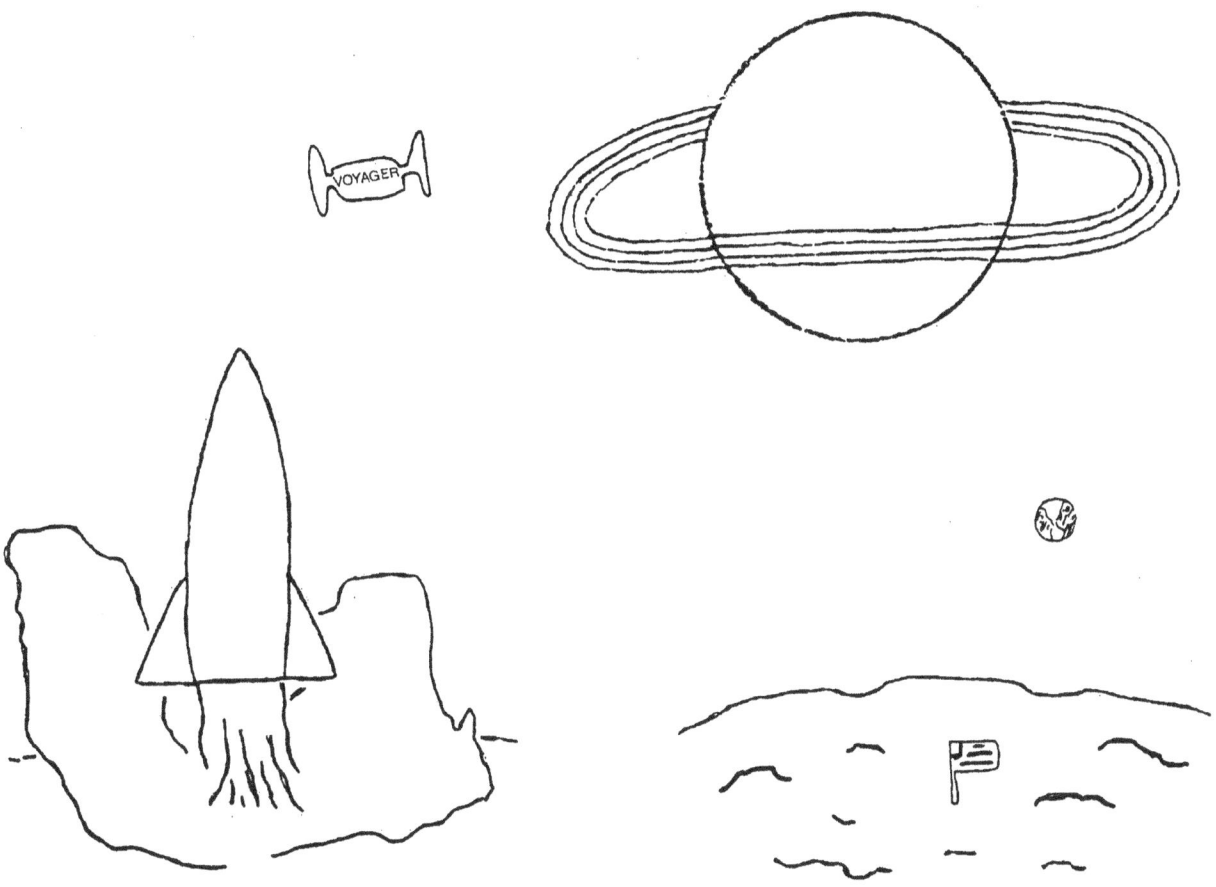

1. Which of the following concepts is common to all of the illustrations shown above? 1.____

    A. Astronomy
    B. Planets
    C. Solar System
    D. Space Exploration

Read the passage preceding Question 2. Then, choose the one best answer based on the information given in the passage.

The safety of the victim at an emergency location is of primary interest. Your first decision may be to move the victim out of danger to prevent further injury or death (for example, from burning buildings, explosive areas, etc.). Once the consciousness or unconsciousness of the victim is determined, your next step is to evaluate the nature and seriousness of the injury. Next, you must assess the emergency first aid that should be administered to the victim and your competence in administering this first aid. Then, you must determine the additional medical assistance you will need at the scene of the emergency.

2. As a police officer you are dispatched to an accident scene involving an injured person. According to the above passage, you should first:

    A. check for bleeding or for broken bones.
    B. check area surrounding victim for evidence.
    C. check for breathing if victim appears to be choking.
    D. determine if victim is in danger of further injury.

2.____

KEY (CORRECT ANSWERS)

1. D
2. D

EXAMINATION SECTION
TEST 1

DIRECTIONS: Each question or incomplete statement is followed by several suggested answers or completions. Select the one that BEST answers the question or completes the statement. *PRINT THE LETTER OF THE CORRECT ANSWER IN THE SPACE AT THE RIGHT.*

Questions 1-10.   MEMORY

DIRECTIONS: Questions 1 through 10 are to be answered SOLELY on the basis of the following passage, which contains a story about an incident involving police officers. You will have ten minutes to read and study the story. You may not write or make any notes while studying it. After ten minutes, close the memory booklet and do not look at it again. Then, answer the questions that follow.

You are one of a number of police officers who have been assigned to help control a demonstration inside Baldwin Square, a major square in the city. The demonstration is to protest the U.S. involvement in Iraq. As was expected, the demonstration has become nasty. You and nine other officers have been assigned to keep the demonstrators from going up Bell Street which enters the Square from the northwest. During the time you have been assigned to Bell Street, you have observed a number of things.

Before the demonstration began, three vans and a wagon entered the Square from the North on Howard Avenue. The first van was a 1989 blue Ford, plate number 897-JLK. The second van was a 1995 red Ford, plate number 899-LKK. The third van was a 1997 green Dodge step-van, plate number 997-KJL. The wagon was a blue 1998 Volvo with a luggage rack on the roof, plate number 989-LKK. The Dodge had a large dent in the left-hand rear door and was missing its radiator grill. The Ford that was painted red had markings under the paint which made you believe that it had once been a telephone company truck. Equipment for the speakers' platform was unloaded from the van, along with a number of demonstration signs. As soon as the vans and wagon were unloaded, a number of demonstrators picked up the signs and started marching around the square. A sign reading *U.S. Out Now* was carried by a woman wearing red jeans, a black tee shirt, and blue sneakers. A man with a beard, a blue shirt, and Army pants began carrying a poster reading *To Hell With Davis*. A tall, Black male and a Hispanic male had been carrying a large sign with *This Is How Vietnam Started* in big black letters with red dripping off the bottom of each letter.

A number of the demonstrators are wearing black armbands and green tee shirts with the peace symbol on the front. A woman with very short hair who was dressed in green and yellow fatigues is carrying a triangular-shaped blue sign with white letters. The sign says *Out Of Iraq*.

A group of 12 demonstrators have been carrying six fake coffins back and forth across the Square between Apple Street on the West and Webb Street on the East. They are shouting *Death to Hollis and his Henchmen*. Over where Victor Avenue enters the Square from the South, a small group of demonstrators (two men and three women) just started painting slogans on the walls surrounding the construction of the First National Union Bank and Trust.

2 (#1)

1. Which street is on the opposite side of the Square from Victor Avenue?   1._____
   A. Bell   B. Howard   C. Apple   D. Webb

2. How many officers are assigned with you?   2._____
   A. 8   B. 6   C. 9   D. 5

3. Howard Avenue enters the Square from which direction?   3._____
   A. Northwest   B. North   C. East   D. Southwest

4. The van that had PROBABLY been a telephone truck had plate number   4._____
   A. 899-LKK   B. 989-LKK   C. 897-JKL   D. 997-KJL

5. What is the color of the sign carried by the woman with very short hair?   5._____
   A. Blue   B. White   C. Black   D. Red

6. The man wearing the army pants has a(n)   6._____
   A. Afro   B. beard
   C. triangular-shaped sign   D. black armband

7. Which vehicle had plate number 989-LKK? The   7._____
   A. red Ford   B. blue Ford   C. Volvo   D. Dodge

8. The bank under construction is located _____ of the Square.   8._____
   A. north   B. south   C. east   D. west

9. How many people are painting slogans on the walls surrounding the construction site?   9._____
   A. 4   B. 5   C. 6   D. 7

10. What is the name of the bank under construction?   10._____
    A. National Union Bank and Trust
    B. First National Bank and Trust
    C. First Union National Bank and Trust
    D. First National Union Bank and Trust

KEY (CORRECT ANSWERS)

1. B   6. B
2. C   7. C
3. B   8. B
4. A   9. B
5. A   10. D

TEST 2

DIRECTIONS: Each question or incomplete statement is followed by several suggested answers or completions. Select the one that BEST answers the question or completes the statement. *PRINT THE LETTER OF THE CORRECT ANSWER IN THE SPACE AT THE RIGHT.*

Questions 1-15.

DIRECTIONS: Questions 1 through 15 are to be answered SOLELY on the basis of the Memory Booklet given below.

MEMORY BOOKLET

The following passage contains a story about an incident involving police officers. You will have ten minutes to read and study the story. You may not write or make any notes while studying it. The first questions in the examination will be based on the passage. After ten minutes, close the memory booklet, and do not look at it again. Then, answer the questions that follow.

Police Officers Boggs and Thomas are patrolling in a radio squad car on a late Saturday afternoon in the spring. They are told by radio that a burglary is taking place on the top floor of a six-story building on the corner of 5th Street and Essex and that they should deal with the incident.

The police officers know the location and know that the Gold Jewelry Company occupies the entire sixth floor. They also know that, over the weekends, the owner has gold bricks in his office safe worth $500,000.

When the officers arrive at the location, they lock their radio car. They then find the superintendent of the building who opens the front door for them. He indicates he has neither seen nor heard anything suspicious in the building. However, he had just returned from a long lunch hour. The officers take the elevator to the sixth floor. As the door of the elevator with the officers opens on the sixth floor, the officers hear the door of the freight elevator in the rear of the building closing and the freight elevator beginning to move. They leave the elevator and proceed quickly through the open door of the office of the Gold Jewelry Company. They see that the office safe is open and empty. The officers quickly proceed to the rear staircase. They run down six flights of stairs, and they see four suspects leaving through the rear entrance of the building.

They run through the rear door and out of the building after the suspects. The four suspects are running quickly through the parking lot at the back of the building. The suspects then make a right-hand turn onto 5th Street and are clearly seen by the officers. The officers see one white male, one Hispanic male, one Black male, and one white female.

The white male has a beard and sunglasses. He is wearing blue jeans, a dark red and blue jacket, and white jogging shoes. He is carrying a large green duffel bag over his shoulder.

The Hispanic male limps slightly and has a dark moustache. He is wearing dark brown slacks, a dark green sweat shirt, and brown shoes. He is carrying a large blue duffel bag.

The Black male is clean-shaven, wearing black corduroy pants, a multi-colored shirt, a green beret, and black boots. He is carrying a tool box.

The white female has long dark hair and is wear-ing light-colored blue jeans, a white blouse, sneakers, and a red kerchief around her neck. She is carrying a shotgun.

The officers chase the suspects for three long blocks without getting any closer to them. At the intersection of 5th Street and Pennsylvania Avenue, the suspects separate. The white male and the Black male rapidly get into a 1992 brown Ford stationwagon. The stationwagon has a roof rack on top and a Connecticut license plate with the letters *JEAN* on it. The stationwagon departs even before the occupants close the door completely.

The Hispanic male and the white female get into an old blue Dodge van. The van has a CB antenna on top, a picture of a cougar on the back doors, a dented right rear fender, and a New Jersey license plate. The officers are not able to read the plate numbers on the van.

The officers then observe the stationwagon turn left and enter an expressway going to Connecticut. The van turns right onto Illinois Avenue and proceeds toward the tunnel to New Jersey.

The officers immediately run back to their radio car to radio in what happened.

1. Which one of the following suspects had sunglasses on?   1.____

    A. White male
    C. Black male
    B. Hispanic male
    D. White female

2. Which one of the following suspects was carrying a shotgun?   2.____

    A. White male
    C. Black male
    B. Hispanic male
    D. White female

3. Which one of the following suspects was wearing a green beret?   3.____

    A. White male
    C. Black male
    B. Hispanic male
    D. White femal

4. Which one of the following suspects limped slightly?   4.____

    A. White male
    C. Black male
    B. Hispanic male
    D. White female

5. Which one of the following BEST describes the stationwagon used?   5.____
    A

    A. 1992 brown Ford
    C. 1979 brown Ford
    B. 1992 blue Dodge
    D. 1979 blue Dodge

6. Which one of the following BEST describes the suspect or suspects who used the stationwagon?
   A

   A. Black male and a Hispanic male
   B. white male and a Hispanic male
   C. Black male and a white male
   D. Black male and a white female

7. The van had a license plate from which of the following states?

   A. Connecticut   B. New Jersey
   C. New York   D. Pennsylvania

8. The license plate on the stationwagon read as follows:

   A. JANE   B. JOAN   C. JEAN   D. JUNE

9. The van used had a dented _____ fender.

   A. left rear   B. right rear
   C. right front   D. left front

10. When last seen by the officers, the van was headed toward

    A. Connecticut   B. New Jersey
    C. Pennsylvania   D. Long Island

11. The female suspect's hair can BEST be described as

    A. long and dark-colored   B. short and dark-colored
    C. long and light-colored   D. short and light-colored

12. Which one of the following suspects was wearing a multicolored shirt?

    A. White male   B. Hispanic male
    C. Black male   D. White female

13. Blue jeans were worn by the _____ male suspect and the suspect.

    A. Hispanic; white female   B. Black; Hispanic male
    C. white; white female   D. Black; white male

14. The color of the duffel bag carried by the Hispanic male suspect was

    A. blue   B. green   C. brown   D. red

15. The Hispanic male suspect was wearing

    A. brown shoes   B. black shoes
    C. black boots   D. jogging shoes

KEY (CORRECT ANSWERS)

1. A
2. D
3. C
4. B
5. A

6. C
7. B
8. C
9. B
10. B

11. A
12. C
13. C
14. A
15. A

READING COMPREHENSION
UNDERSTANDING WRITTEN MATERIALS
COMMENTARY

The ability to read and understand written materials—texts, publications, newspapers, orders, directions, expositions—is a skill basic to a functioning democracy and to an efficient business or viable government.

That is why almost all examinations—for beginning, middle, and senior levels—test reading comprehension, directly or indirectly.

The reading test measures how well you understand what you read. This is how it is done: You read a passage followed by several statements. From these statements, you choose the one statement, or answer, that is BEST supported by, or BEST matches, what is said in the paragraph. PRINT THE LETTER OF THE CORRECT ANSWER IN THE SPACE AT THE RIGHT.

SAMPLE QUESTIONS

DIRECTIONS: Answer Questions 1 and 2 ONLY according to the information given in the following passage.

1. When a fingerprint technician inks and takes rolled impressions of a subject's fingers, the degree of downward pressure the technician applies is important. The correct pressure may best be determined through experience and observation. It is quite important, however, that the subject be cautioned to relax and not help the fingerprint technician by also applying pressure, as this prevents the fingerprint technician from gaging the amount needed. A method which is helpful in getting the subject to relax his hand is to instruct him to look at some distant object and not to look at his hands.

1. According to this passage, the technician tries to relax the subject's hands by   1._____
   A. instructing him to let his hands hang loosely
   B. telling him that being fingerprinted is painless
   C. asking him to look at this hand instead of some distant object
   D. asking him to look at something other than his hand

2. The subject is asked NOT to press down on his fingers while being fingerprinted   2._____
   because
   A. the impressions taken become rolled
   B. the subject may apply too little downward pressure and spoil the impressions
   C. the technician cannot tell whether he is applying the right degree of pressure
   D. he doesn't have the experience to apply the exact amount of pressure

CORRECT ANSWERS
1. D
2. C

EXAMINATION SECTION
TEST 1

DIRECTIONS: Questions 1 through 3 are to be answered on the basis of the following reading passage. *PRINT THE LETTER OF THE CORRECT ANSWER IN THE SPACE AT THE RIGHT.*

Thermostats should be tested in hot water for proper opening. A bucket should be filled with sufficient water to cover the thermostat and fitted with a thermometer suspended in the water so that the sensitive bulb portion does not rest directly on the bucket. The water is then heated on a stove. As the temperature of the water passes the 160-165° range, the thermostat should start to open and should be completely opened when the temperature has risen to 185-190°. Lifting the thermostat into the air should cause a pronounced closing action and the unit should be closed entirely within a short time.

1. The thermostat described above is a device which opens and closes with changes in the
    A. position   B. pressure   C. temperature   D. surroundings

    1.____

2. According to the above passage, the closing action of the thermostat should be tested by
    A. working the thermostat back and forth
    B. permitting the water to cool gradually
    C. adding cold water to the bucket
    D. removing the thermostat from the bucket

    2.____

3. The bulb of the thermometer should not rest directly on the bucket because
    A. the bucket gets hotter than the water
    B. the thermometer might be damaged in that position
    C. it is difficult to read the thermometer in that position
    D. the thermometer might interfere with operation of the thermostat

    3.____

KEY (CORRECT ANSWERS)

1. C
2. D
3. A

TEST 2

DIRECTIONS: Questions 1 through 3 are to be answered on the basis of the following reading passage. *PRINT THE LETTER OF THE CORRECT ANSWER IN THE SPACE AT THE RIGHT.*

All idle pumps should be turned daily by hand, and should be run under power at least once a week. Whenever repairs are made on a pump, a record should be kept so that it will be possible to judge the success with which the pump is performing its functions. If a pump fails to deliver liquid, there may be an obstruction in the suction line, the pump's parts may be badly worn, or the packing defective.

1. According to the above passage, pumps 1._____
   A. in use should be turned by hand every day
   B. which are not in use should be run under power every day
   C. which are in daily use should be run under power several times a week
   D. which are not in use should be turned by hand every day

2. According to the above passage, the reason for keeping records of repairs made on pumps is to 2._____
   A. make certain that proper maintenance is being performed
   B. discover who is responsible for improper repairs
   C. rate the performance of the pumps
   D. know when to replace worn parts

3. The one of the following causes of pump failure which is NOT mentioned in the above passage is 3._____
   A. excessive suction lift   B. clogged lines
   C. bad packing   D. worn parts

KEY (CORRECT ANSWERS)

1. A
2. C
3. A

TEST 3

DIRECTIONS: Questions 1 through 5 are to be answered on the basis of the following reading passage. *PRINT THE LETTER OF THE CORRECT ANSWER IN THE SPACE AT THE RIGHT.*

Floors in warehouses, storerooms, and shipping rooms must be strong enough to stay level under heavy loads. Unevenness of floors may cause boxes of materials to topple and fall. Safe floor load capacities and maximum heights to which boxes may be stacked should be posted conspicuously so all can notice it. Where material in boxes, containers, or cartons of the same weight is regularly stored, it is good practice to paint a horizontal line on the wall indicating the maximum height to which the material may be piled. A qualified expert should determine floor load capacity from the building plans, the age and condition of the floor supports, the type of floor, and other related information.

Working aisles are those from which material is placed into and removed from storage. Working aisles are of two types: transportation aisles, running the length of the building, and cross aisles, running across the width of the building. Deciding on the number, width, and location of working aisles is important. While aisles are necessary and determine boundaries of storage areas, they reduce the space actually used for storage.

1. According to the above passage, how should safe floor load capacities be made known to employees? They should be
   A. given out to each employee
   B. given to supervisors only
   C. printed in large red letters
   D. posted so that they are easily seen

   1._____

2. According to the above passage, floor load capacities should be determined by
   A. warehouse supervisors   B. the fire department
   C. qualified experts   D. machine operators

   2._____

3. According to the above passage, transportation aisles
   A. run the length of the building
   B. run across the width of the building
   C. are wider than cross aisles
   D. are shorter than cross aisles

   3._____

4. According to the above passage, working aisles tend to
   A. take away space that could be used for storage
   B. add to space that could be used for storage
   C. slow down incoming stock
   D. speed up outgoing stock

   4._____

5. According to the above passage, unevenness of floors may cause
   A. overall warehouse deterioration   B. piles of stock to fall
   C. materials to spoil   D. many worker injuries

   5._____

KEY (CORRECT ANSWERS)

1. D
2. C
3. A
4. A
5. B

TEST 4

DIRECTIONS: Questions 1 through 3 are to be answered on the basis of the following reading passage. *PRINT THE LETTER OF THE CORRECT ANSWER IN THE SPACE AT THE RIGHT.*

In a retail establishment, any overweight means a distinct loss to the merchant, and even an apparently inconsequential overweight on a single package or sale when multiplied by the total number of transactions, could run into large figures. In addition to the use of reliable scales and weights, and their maintenance in proper condition, there must be proper supervision of the selling force. Such supervision is a difficult matter, particularly on the score of carelessness, as the depositing of extra amounts of material on the scale and failure to remove the same when it overbalances the scale may become a habit. In case of underweight, either in the weighing or by the use of fraudulent scales and weights, the seller soon will hear of it, but there is no reason why the amount weighed out should be in excess of what the customer pays for. Checking sales records against invoices and inventories can supply some indication of the tendency of the sales force to become careless in this field.

1. Of the following, the MOST valid implication of the above passage is that
    A. all overweights which occur in retail stores are in small amounts
    B. even-arm and uneven-arm balances and weights which are unreliable lead more often to underweights than to overweights
    C. overweights due to errors of salesclerks necessarily lead to large losses by a retailer
    D. supervision to prevent overweights is more important to a retailer than remedial measures after their occurrence

1.____

2. Of the following, the MOST valid implication of the above passage is that
    A. depositing of insufficient amounts of commodities on scales and failure to add to them may become a habit with salesclerks
    B. salesclerks should be trained in understanding and maintenance of scale mechanisms
    C. supervision of salesclerks to prevent careless habits in weighing must depend upon personal observation

2.____

3. According to the above passage, the MOST accurate of the following statements is:
    A. For the most part, the ideas expressed in the passage do not apply to wholesale establishments.
    B. Inventories of commodities prepacked in the store are the only ones which can be used in checking losses due to overweight.
    C. Invoices which give the value and weight of merchandise received are useful in checking losses due to overweights.
    D. The principal value of inventories is to indicate losses due to overweights.

3.____

KEY (CORRECT ANSWERS)

1. D
2. C
3. C

TEST 5

DIRECTIONS: Questions 1 through 5 are to be answered on the basis of the following reading passage. *PRINT THE LETTER OF THE CORRECT ANSWER IN THE SPACE AT THE RIGHT.*

TITANIC AIR COMPRESSOR

Valves: The compressors are equipped with Titanic plate valves which are automatic in operation. Valves are so constructed that an entire valve assembly can readily be removed from the head. The valves provide large port areas with short lift and are accurately guided to insure positive seating.

Starting Unloader: Each compressor (or air end) is equipped with a centrifugal governor which is bolted directly to the compressor crank shaft. The governor actuates cylinder relief valves so as to relieve pressure from the cylinders during starting and stopping. The motor is never required to start the compressor tinder load.

Air Strainer: Each cylinder air inlet connection is fitted with a suitable combination air strainer and muffler.

Pistons: Pistons are lightweight castings, ribbed internally to secure strength, and are accurately turned and ground. Each piston is fitted with four (4) rings, two of which are oil control rings. Piston pins are hardened and tempered steel of the full floating type. Bronze bushings are used between piston pin and piston

Connecting Rods: Connecting rods are of solid bronze designed for maximum strength, rigidity, and wear. Crank pins are fitted with renewable steel bushings. Connecting rods are of the one-piece type, there being no bolts, nuts, or cotter pins which can come loose. With this type of construction, wear is reduced to a negligible amount, and adjustment of wrist pin and crank pin bearings is unnecessary.

Main Bearings: Main bearings are of the ball type and are securely held in position by spacers. This type of bearing entirely eliminates the necessity of frequent adjustment or attention. The crank shaft is always in perfect alignment.

Crank Shaft: The crank shaft is a one-piece heat-treated forging of best quality open-hearth steel, of rugged design and of sufficient size to transmit the motor power and any additional stresses which may occur in service. Each crank shaft is counter-balanced (dynamically balanced to reduce vibration to a minimum, and is accurately machined to properly receive the ball-bearing races, crank pin bushing, flexible coupling, and centrifugal governor. Suitable provision is made to insure proper lubrication of all crank shaft bearings and bushings with the minimum amount of attention.

Coupling: Compressor and motor shafts are connected through a Morse Chain Company all-metal enclosed flexible coupling. This coupling consists of two sprockets, one mounted on, and keyed to, each shaft; the sprockets are wrapped by a single Morse Chain, the entire assembly being enclosed in a split aluminum grease-packed cover.

1. The crank pin of the connecting rod is fitted with a renewable bushing made of   1.____
    A. solid bronze   B. steel
    C. a lightweight casting   D. ball bearings

2. When the connecting rod is of the one-piece type,
   A. the wrist pins require frequent adjustment
   B. the crank pins require frequent adjustment
   C. the cotter pins frequently will come loose
   D. wear is reduced to a negligible amount

3. The centrifugal governor is bolted directly to the
   A. compressor crank shaft   B. main bearing
   C. piston pin   D. muffler

4. The number of oil control rings required for each piston is
   A. one   B. two   C. three   D. four

5. The compressor and motor shafts are connected through a flexible coupling. These couplings are _____ to the shafts.
   A. keyed   B. brazed   C. soldered   D. press-fit

KEY (CORRECT ANSWERS)

1. B
2. D
3. A
4. B
5. A

TEST 6

DIRECTIONS: Questions 1 through 6 are to be answered on the basis of the following reading passage. *PRINT THE LETTER OF THE CORRECT ANSWER IN THE SPACE AT THE RIGHT.*

Perhaps the strongest argument the mass transit backer has is the advantage in efficiency that mass transit has over the automobile in the urban traffic picture. It has been estimated that given comparable location and construction conditions, the subway can carry four times as many passengers per hour and cost half as much to build as urban highways. Yet public apathy regarding the mass transportation movement in the 1960's resulted in the building of more roads. Planned to provide 42,000 miles of highways in the period from 1956-72, including 7,500 miles within cities, the Federal Highway System project is now about two-thirds completed. The Highway Trust Fund supplies 90 percent of the cost of the system, with state and local sources putting up the rest of the money. By contrast, a municipality as had to put up the bulk of the cost of a rapid transit system. Although the system and its Trust Fund have come under attack in the past few years from environmentalists and groups opposed to the continued building of urban freeways—considered to be the most expensive, destructive, and inefficient segments of the system—a move by them to get the Trust Fund transformed into a general transportation fund at the expiration of the present program in 1972 seems to be headed nowhere.

1. Given similar building conditions and locations, a city that builds a subway instead of a highway can expect to receive for each dollar spent _____ as much transport value.
   A. half   B. twice   C. four times   D. eight times

2. The general attitude of the public in the past ten years toward the mass transportation movement has been
   A. favorable   B. indifferent   C. enthusiastic   D. unfriendly

3. The number of miles of highways still to be completed in the Federal Highway System project is MOST NEARLY
   A. 2,500   B. 5,000   C. 14,000   D. 28,000

4. What do certain groups who object to some features of the Federal Highway System program want to do with the Highway Trust Fund after 1972?
   A. Extend it in order to complete the project
   B. Change it so that the money can be used for all types of transportation
   C. End it even if the project is not completed
   D. Change it so that the money will be used only for urban freeways

5. Which one of the following statements is a VALID conclusion based on the facts in the above passage?
   A. The advantage of greater efficiency is the only argument that supporters of the mass transportation movement can offer.
   B. It was easier for cities to build roads rather than mass transit systems in the last 15 years because of the large financial contribution made by the Federal Government.

    C. Mass transit systems cause as much congestion and air pollution in cities as automobiles.
    D. In 1972, the Highway Trust Fund becomes a general transportation fund.

6. The MAIN idea or theme of the above passage is that the   6.____
    A. cost of the Federal Highway System is shared by the federal, state, and local governments
    B. public is against spending money for building mass transportation facilities in the cities
    C. cities would benefit more from expansion and improvement of their mass transit systems than from the building of more highways
    D. building of mass transportation facilities has been slowed by the Highway Trust Fund

KEY (CORRECT ANSWERS)

1. D
2. B
3. C
4. B
5. B
6. C

TEST 7

DIRECTIONS: Questions 1 through 5 are to be answered on the basis of the following reading passage. *PRINT THE LETTER OF THE CORRECT ANSWER IN THE SPACE AT THE RIGHT.*

The use of role-playing as a training technique was developed during the past decade by social scientists, particularly psychologists, who have been active in training experiments. Originally, this technique was applied by clinical psychologists who discovered that a patient appears to gain understanding of an emotionally disturbing situation when encouraged to act out roles in that situation. As applied in government and business organizations, the purpose of role-playing is to aid employees to understand certain work problems involving interpersonal relations and to enable observers to evaluate various reactions to them. Thus, for example, on the problem of handling grievances, two individuals from the group might be selected to act out extemporaneously the parts of subordinate and supervisor. When this situation is enacted by various pairs among the class and the techniques and results are discussed, the members of the group are presumed to reach conclusions about the most effective means of handling similar situations. Often the use or role reversal, where participants take parts different from their actual work roles, assists individuals to gain more insight into other people's problems and viewpoints. Although role-playing can be a rewarding training device, the trainer must be aware of his responsibilities. If this technique is to be successful, thorough briefing of both actors and observers as to the situation in question, the participants' roles, and what to look for, is essential.

1. The role-playing technique was FIRST used for the purpose of
    A. measuring the effectiveness of training programs
    B. training supervisors in business organizations
    C. treating emotionally disturbed patients
    D. handling employee grievances

    1.____

2. When role-playing is used in private business as a training device, the CHIEF aim is to
    A. develop better relations between supervisor and subordinate in the handling of grievances
    B. come up with a solution to a specific problem that has arisen
    C. determine the training needs of the group
    D. increase employee understanding of the human-relation factors in work situations

    2.____

3. From the above passage, it is MOST reasonable to conclude that when role-playing is used, it is preferable to have the roles acted out by
    A. only one set of actors
    B. no more than two sets of actors
    C. several different sets of actors
    D. the trainer or trainers of the group

    3.____

4. It can be inferred from the above passage that a limitation of role-playing as a training method is that
   A. many work situations do not lend themselves to role-play
   B. employees are not experienced enough as actors to play the roles realistically
   C. only trainers who have psychological training can use it successfully
   D. participants who are observing and not acting do not benefit from it

5. To obtain *good* results from the use of role-play in training, a trainer should give participants
   A. a minimum of information about the situation so that they can act spontaneously
   B. scripts which illustrate the best method for handling the situation
   C. a complete explanation of the problem and the roles to be acted out
   D. a summary of work problems which involve interpersonal relations

KEY (CORRECT ANSWERS)

1. C
2. D
3. C
4. A
5. C

EXAMINATION SECTION
TEST 1

DIRECTIONS: Each question or incomplete statement is followed by several suggested answers or completions. Select the one that BEST answers the question or completes the statement. *PRINT THE LETTER OF THE CORRECT ANSWER IN THE SPACE AT THE RIGHT.*

QUESTIONS 1-4.

Questions 1-4 refer to the following information.

A recent study shows that of the 1000 graduates of Learnmore High School, 40% claimed that they smoked during their high school years, 30% said they started smoking before entering high school and continued smoking during high school years. Of the people who didn't smoke at all during their high school year, 70% claim that they have no medical problems. However, only 10% of those who did smoke during their high school years reported no medical problem.

1. What percent of all these graduates claim they have NO medical problem? 1.____
   - A. 30
   - B. 42
   - C. 60
   - D. 70
   - E. None of the above

2. How many non-smokers have had at LEAST one medical problem? 2.____
   - A. 70   B. 180   C. 280   D. 350   E. 450

3. What is the MAXIMUM number of people who began smoking before entering high school, and have had NO medical problems? 3.____
   - A. 10   B. 30   C. 40   D. 100   E. over 100

4. Counting only individuals who have experienced at least one medical problem, what is the ratio of those who didn't smoke during high school years to those who did smoke during that time period? 4.____
   - A. 3:2   B. 1:2   C. 1:3   D. 2:3   E. 3:1

5. If John enjoys the taste of pineapple, he'll like the taste of all fruit. The preceding statement is MOST similar to which of the following? 5.____
   - A. If a dog has a liking for human food, he'll like all dog food
   - B. If a person can understand algebra, he can understand all mathematics
   - C. If a Chevrolet gets good gas mileage, then so will a Datsun
   - D. If Sue's favorite color is red, then she won't buy a green dress
   - E. If Bob can fix any electrical item, then he can fix a toaster

6. Only a few people who are heavy smokers will live past the age of 90. Since Eve is a 30-year-old non-smoker, she will probably live beyond the age of 90. 6.____
   The argument is MOST similar to which of the following?

55

A. Only a few cities like Cleanville have a low crime rate. Thus, if a person lives in a low crime rate city, that city must be Cleanville.
B. Only birds have feathers. Thus, some birds have morefeathers than other birds.
C. All weight-lifters are light sleepers. Since Bob is a heavy sleeper, he doesn't lift weights.
D. Not many individuals who worry a lot can get a good night's rest. Since John does not worry at all, he can probably get a good night's rest.
E. Some mathematicians enjoy all sports. Since William is a mathematician, he may not enjoy any sports.

7. Since Jack is left-handed, he is an excellent tennis player. Assuming that the preceding statement is true, from which one(s) of the following can this quoted statement be logically deduced?
    I. All tennis players are left-handed.
    II. None of the excellent tennis players is right-handed.
    III. Either Jack is right-handed or he is an excellent tennis player.

    A. I only   B. II only   C. III only
    D. II and III   E. I, II, and III

8. Gamblers are boisterous individuals. Yesterday, I went to the racetrack and there was a lot of shouting after every race. The above argument assumes:
    I. Gamblers frequent racetracks.
    II. Noisy people are gamblers.
    III. Quiet people don't go to racetracks.

    A. I only   B. II only   C. III only
    D. I, III   E. I, II, III

QUESTIONS 9-14.

Questions 9-14 refer to the facts below. It is to be assumed that it is the month of July, the first day of which is a Monday.

The Ail-Weather appliance store sells televisions, radios, toasters, and refrigerators. Certain conditions govern this store:

I. The store is open only Monday through Friday every month. Thus, all purchases and deliveries can only be made Monday through Friday.
II. TV's and radios are only delivered on even numbered days.
III. Refrigerators are delivered only on Tuesdays and Thursdays.
IV. Toasters are delivered on any date of the month which can be divided evenly by 3 or 5.
V. A customer may purchase a radio or a toaster on the day of delivery.
VI. Since refrigerators and TV's are more expensive items, they are immediately inspected on the day of delivery. However, a customer may not purchase these items until 3 business days after delivery.

9. Which item(s) could be neither delivered nor purchased on Wednesdays?

    A. TV's and radios   B. TV's, radios, and refrigerators
    C. Refrigerators and toasters   D. Refrigerators *only*
    E. Toasters *only*

10. On how many days during this month can toasters be purchased?

    A. At least 4 but fewer than 7   B. 9
    C. 11   D. More than 11
    E. None of the above

11. During the first week, on which dates may a TV either be purchased or delivered?

    A. 2nd, 3rd, 4th   B. 2nd, 4th, 5th   C. 3rd, 4th, 5th
    D. 2nd, 5th, 6th   E. 2nd, 3rd

12. On how many days during this month can TV's be delivered?

    A. Fewer than 6   B. 8   C. 9
    D. 10   E. 11

13. What is the *earliest* date on which both a TV and toaster can be purchased?

    A. 3rd   B. 5th   C. 7th   D. 9th   E. 11th

14. Which appliance(s) has(have) exactly 2 delivery dates on Fridays?

    A. Toasters, radios, TV's   B. Toasters, TV's
    C. TV's, radios   D. Toasters, radios
    E. Only toasters

15. If a person studies hard, he can pass any high school course.
    This statement can be logically deduced from which of the following?

    A. Some people study while others don't study.
    B. A person who has passed a particular high school course must have studied hard.
    C. A high school course can be passed if a person is willing to study hard.
    D. If a person doesn't study, he can't expect to pass a high school course.
    E. Some high school courses require more studying than do other courses.

QUESTIONS 16-17.

Questions 16 and 17 are to be answered on the basis of the following.

The most dangerous sport in the world is thoroughbred horseracing, since more participants per thousand are killed than in any other sport. Hang-gliding is the second most dangerous sport. By contrast, boxing ranks tenth on the list of most dangerous sports.

16. The author of the above paragraph is *most likely* trying to convey the message that:

    A. Most sports are dangerous
    B. Hang-gliding is popular despite its danger
    C. Only ten sports are considered dangerous
    D. The most number of injuries occur in horseracing
    E. Boxing is not the most dangerous sport

17. The author would *probably* be opposed to:

    A. Any dangerous sport
    B. A ban on boxing
    C. Amateur boxing
    D. Horseracing
    E. A ban on horseracing

QUESTIONS 18-22.

Questions 18-22 are to be answered on the basis of the following.
The Expanding Food Company has outlet stores on each of First Ave., Second Ave., Third Ave., Fourth Ave., and Fifth Ave. Also, it is known that:

   I. There is at least one store on each avenue.
   II. The number of stores on Fifth Ave. equals the sum of the number of stores on First Ave. plus those on Second Ave.
   III. The number of stores on Second Ave. is double the number of stores on Third Ave.
   IV. The number of stores on Fourth Ave. is greater than the number of stores on Fifth Ave.
   V. There are an even number of stores on First Ave.

18. What is the *fewest* number of stores that must exist on Fourth Ave.?

    A. 2   B. 3   C. 4   D. 5   E. 6

19. Which avenue has the MOST stores?

    A. Fifth Ave.   B. Fourth Ave.
    C. Third Ave.   D. All of the above
    E. None of the above

20. Suppose NO avenue has *more* than 7 stores. Find the total number of stores on all 5 avenues.

    A. 16 or 19   B. 20
    C. 21   D. 16, 19 or 20
    E. 16, 20 or 21

21. The number of stores on Fifth Ave

    A. must be even
    B. must be odd
    C. could equal the number of stores on First Ave.
    D. could equal the number of stores on Second Ave.
    E. none of the above

22. Suppose it is known that there are 4 stores on Third Ave. and that there are *more* than 4 stores on First Ave.
    Find the *minimum* number of stores on all 5 avenues.

    A. 45   B. 49   C. 46   D. 48   E. 47

QUESTIONS 23-25.

Questions 23 through 25 are to be answered on the basis of the following.

In a particular group of 21 people, each individual is one of three professions: doctor, engineer, or teacher. Half the number of people who smoke are engineers. One-third of the number of non-smokers are doctors. The number of engineers who smoke equals the number of non-smokers who are not doctors.

23. How many of the non-smokers are doctors?

    A. 2 B. 3 C. 5 D. 6 E. 9

24. If all the teachers are smokers, and there are only 2 doctors who smoke, then the teachers represent _____ Percent of the entire group.

    A. 19 B. 25 C. 29 D. 33 E. 40

25. Using the information from the preceding question, *how many* engineers are there in the entire group?

    A. 3 B. 6 C. 9 D. 12 E. 15

KEY (CORRECT ANSWERS)

1. E		11. B	
2. B		12. E	
3. C		13. B	
4. B		14. A	
5. B		15. C	
6. D		16. E	
7. C		17. B	
8. A		18. D	
9. D		19. B	
10. E		20. E	

21. A
22. E
23. B
24. A
25. D

SOLUTIONS

1. (.70)(.60) = .42 of all the graduates didn't smoke and didn't have any medical problems, whereas (.10)(.40) = .04 of all the graduates did smoke but yet didn't experience any medical problems. Thus, .42 + .04 = .46 or 46% of all graduates claimed they had no medical problems.

   (ANSWER E).

2. (.30)(.60) = .18 of the population were non-smokers and yet had at least one medical problem. Now (.18)(1000) = 180.

   (ANSWER B).

3. (.10)(.40) = .04 indicates the number of people who did smoke during their high school years and had no medical problem. Of the .04, it is not possible to determine what fraction actually started smoking before entering high school. So, (.04)(1000) = 40.

   (ANSWER C).

4. (.30)(.60) = .18 of the non-smokers had at least one medical problem, whereas (.90)(.40) = .36 of the smokers had at least one medical problem. Then .18/.36 = 1:2 ratio.

   (ANSWER B).

5. The original statement uses the truth of a specific item in order to imply the truth of a general item containing that specific item. Only choice B illustrates that kind of reasoning.

   (ANSWER B).

6. The original statement can be written: "If A, then B. If not A, then not B." This argument is not necessarily valid, but choice D resembles it most closely.

   (ANSWER D).

7. Statement I is false, since we can assume that there exist both left-handed and right-handed players. Statement II is also false, because there may be excellent right-handed players. Statement III is true, since Jack is not right-handed and thus would have to be an excellent tennis player.

   (ANSWER C).

8. The only valid implication is Statement I, since one can assume that gamblers do visit racetracks. (This statement could be false, since it is only an assumption). Statement II is not valid since many types of people are noisy. Statement III is also invalid since one can assume that both noisy and quiet people frequent racetracks.

   (ANSWER A).

QUESTIONS 9-14.

Questions 9-14 see calendars below showing days of receiving and purchasing of each of the 4 different appliances. Note that for question #10, the actual answer is 10.

7 (#1)

Radio Delivered / TV Delivered

Sun	Mon	Tu	Wed	Th	Fri	Sat
	1	②	3	④	5	6
7	⑧	9	⑩	11	⑫	13
14	15	⑯	17	⑱	19	20
21	㉒	23	㉔	25	㉖	27
28	29	㉚	31			

Toaster Delivered

Sun	Mon	Tu	Wed	Th	Fri	Sat
	1	2	③	4	⑤	6
7	8	⑨	⑩	11	⑫	13
14	⑮	16	17	⑱	19	20
21	22	23	㉔	㉕	26	27
28	29	㉚	31			

Refrigerator Delivered

Sun	Mon	Tu	Wed	Th	Fri	Sat
	1	②	3	④	5	6
7	8	⑨	10	⑪	12	13
14	15	⑯	17	⑱	19	20
21	22	㉓	24	㉕	26	27
28	29	㉚	31			

Radio Purchased

Sun	Mon	Tu	Wed	Th	Fri	Sat
	1	②	3	④	5	6
7	⑧	9	⑩	11	⑫	13
14	15	⑯	17	⑱	19	20
21	㉒	23	㉔	25	㉖	27
28	29	㉚	31			

8 (#1)

Radio Purchased

Sun	Mon	Tu	Wed	Th	Fri	Sat
	1	②	3	④	5	6
7	⑧	9	⑩	11	⑫	13
14	15	⑯	17	⑱	19	20
21	㉒	23	㉔	25	㉖	27
28	29	㉚	31			

Toaster Purchased

Sun	Mon	Tu	Wed	Th	Fri	Sat
	1	2	③	4	⑤	6
7	8	⑨	⑩	11	⑫	13
14	⑮	16	17	⑱	19	20
21	22	23	㉔	㉕	26	27
28	29	㉚	31			

TV Purchased

Sun	Mon	Tu	Wed	Th	Fri	Sat
	1	2	3	4	⑤	6
7	8	⑨	10	⑪	12	13
14	⑮	16	⑰	18		20
21	22	㉓	24	㉕	26	27
28	㉙	30	㉛			

Refrigerator Purchased

Sun	Mon	Tu	Wed	Th	Fri	Sat
	1	2	3	4	⑤	6
7	8	⑨	10	11	⑫	13
14	15	⑯	17	18	⑲	20
21	22	㉓	24	25	㉖	27
28	29	㉚	31			

9. (ANSWER D).

10. (ANSWER E).

11. (ANSWER B).

12. (ANSWER E).

13. (ANSWER B).

14. (ANSWER A).

15. The original statement follows logically from choice C, since it implies that studying hard is a prerequisite to passing any high school course.

    (ANSWER C).

16. Although the general public perceives boxing as the most dangerous sport(or at least one of the most dangerous), the author is relying on a certain type of statistic to illustrate that there are nine other sports which could be considered more dangerous than boxing.

    (ANSWER E).

17. The author, by his argument, appears to be defending any ban on the sport of boxing. He does not make any case for or against another sport.

    (ANSWER B).

18. Let x, $2y$, y, w, z be the number of stores respectively on First, Second, Third, Fourth, and Fifth Avenues. Also, $z = x + 2y$, $w > z$, and x must be an even number. Since the smallest values for x and y are 2 and 1 respectively, the minimum value of $z = 2 + (2)(1) = 4$. Now w = the number of stores on Fourth Ave., and since $w > z$, then $w > 4$. Thus, 5 is the minimum value of w.

    (ANSWER D).

19. Since $z = x + 2y$, $z > x$ and $z > y$. But $w > z$, so that w is the variable with the highest value. We know that w = the number of stores on Fourth Ave.

    (ANSWER B).

20. Assume $z = 7$. Then there are two e possible combinations of numbers associated with the number of stores on First, Second, Third, Fourth, and Fifth Avenues respectively. The 1st combination is 2, 4, 2, 7, 6; the 2nd combination is 4, 2, 1, 7, 6; the 3rd combination is 2, 2, 1, 7, 4. Thus, only 16, 20, or 21 are the possible totals.

    (ANSWER E).

21. Since $z = x + 2y$ and x must be even, then z must also be an even number. Note that $2y$ is already even. Thus, even number + even number = even number.

    (ANSWER A).

22. Since Third Ave. has 4 stores, Second Ave. has 8 stores. We also know that First Ave. has more than 4 stores; thus it must have a minimum of 6 stores (even number). Fifth Ave. has $6 + 8 = 14$ stores at minimum, and 15 = the minimum stores on Fourth Ave. Thus, the number of stores on all 5 avenues (minimum) $= 6 + 8 + 4 + 14 + 15 = 47$.

    (ANSWER E).

23. Let x = # of smokers, so that $21 - x$ = # of non-smokers. Then $1/2x$ = # of smokers who are also engineers. This number must equal the number of non-smokers who are not doctors. We can infer that 2/3 of the non-smokers (i.e. $2/3 [21 - x]$) are not doctors. Thus, $1/2x = 2/3 (21 - x)$. So, $x = 12$ and $21 - x = 9$. This implies that there are a total of 9 non-smokers. Since 1/3 of this number are doctors, there are 3 non-smoking doctors.

(ANSWER B).

24. Since 1/2 of the smokers are engineers, this translates to (1/2)(12) = 6 people. Only 2 doctors smoke, so the number of teachers who smoke = 12 - 6 - 2 = 4. (All teachers are smokers). Now 4/21 = .1905 or approximately 19%.

(ANSWER A).

25. The non-smokers must consist of only doctors and engineers. Of the 9 non-smokers, 3 are doctors. Thus 6 non-smokers are engineers. We already know that there are 6 engineers who smoke, so that there are a total of 12 engineers.

(ANSWER D).

EXAMINATION SECTION

TEST 1

DIRECTIONS: Each question or incomplete statement is followed by several suggested answers or completions. Select the one that BEST answers the question or completes the statement. *PRINT THE LETTER OF THE CORRECT ANSWER IN THE SPACE AT THE RIGHT.*

Questions 1-6.

DIRECTIONS: Questions 1 through 6 are to be answered SOLELY on the basis of the numbered boxes on the Arrest Report and paragraph below.

ARREST REPORT

1. Arrest Number	2. Precinct of Arrest	3. Date/Time of Arrest	4. Defendant's Name		5. Defendant's Address
6. Defendant's Date of Birth	7. Sex	8. Race	9. Height	10. Weight	11. Location of Arrest	12. Date and Time of Occurrence
13. Location of Occurrence	14. Complaint Number		15. Victim's Name		16. Victim's Address	17. Victim's Date of Birth
18. Precinct of Complaint	19. Arresting Officer's Name		20. Shield Number		21. Assigned Unit Precinct	2. Date of Complaint

On Friday, December 13 at 11:45 P.M., while leaving a store at 235 Spring Street, Grace O'Connell, a white female, 5'2" 130 lbs., was approached by a white male, 5'11", 200 lbs., who demanded her money and jewelry. As the man ran and turned down River Street, Police Officer William James, Shield Number 31724, assigned to the 14th Precinct, gave chase and apprehended him in front of 523 River Street. The prisoner, Gerald Grande, who resides at 17 Water Street, was arrested at 12:05 A.M., was charged with robbery, and taken to the 13th Precinct, where he was assigned Arrest Number 53048. Miss O'Connell, who resides at 275 Spring St., was given Complaint Number 822460.

1. On the basis of the Arrest Report and the above paragraph, the CORRECT entry for Box Number 3 should be
   A. 11:45 P.M., 12/13
   B. 11:45 P.M., 12/14
   C. 12:05 A.M., 12/13
   D. 12:05 A.M., 12/14

   1._____

2. On the basis of the Arrest Report and the above paragraph, the CORRECT entry for Box Number 21 should be
   A. 12th Precinct
   B. 14th Precinct
   C. Mounted Unit
   D. 32nd Precinct

   2._____

3. On the basis of the Arrest Report and the above paragraph, the CORRECT entry for Box Number 11 should be
   A. 235 Spring St.
   B. 523 River St.
   C. 275 Spring St.
   D. 17 Water St.

   3._____

4. On the basis of the Arrest Report and the above paragraph, the CORRECT entry for Box Number 2 should be
   A. 13th Precinct
   B. 14th Precinct
   C. Mounted Unit
   D. 32nd Precinct

   4._____

5. On the basis of the Arrest Report and the above paragraph, the CORRECT entry for Box Number 13 should be
   A. 523 River St.
   B. 17 Water St.
   C. 275 Spring St.
   D. 235 Spring St.

   5._____

6. On the basis of the Arrest Report and the above paragraph, the CORRECT entry for Box Number 14 should be
   A. 53048   B. 31724   C. 12/13   D. 82460

   6._____

Questions 7-10.

DIRECTIONS: Questions 7 through 10 are to be answered SOLELY on the basis of the following information.

You are required to file various documents in file drawers which are labeled according to the following pattern:

DOCUMENTS

MEMOS		LETTERS		REPORTS		INQUIRIES	
File	Subject	File	Subject	File	Subject	File	Subject
84PM1	(A-L)	84PC1	(A-L)	84PR1	(A-L)	84PQ1	(A-L)
84PM2	(M-Z)	84PC2	(M-Z)	84PR2	(M-Z)	84PQ2	(M-Z)

7. A letter dealing with a burglary should be filed in the drawer labeled
   A. 84PM1   B. 84PC1   C. 84PR1   D. 84PQ2

   7._____

8. A report on *Statistics* should be found in the drawer labeled
   A. 84PM1   B. 84PC2   C. 84PR2   D. 84PQ2

   8._____

9. An inquiry is received about parade permit procedures. It should be filed in the drawer labeled
   A. 84PM2   B. 84PC1   C. 84PR1   D. 84PQ2

   9._____

10. A police officer has a question about a robbery report you filed. You should pull this file from the drawer labeled
    A. 84PM1   B. 84PM2   C. 84PR1   D. 84PR2

    10._____

Questions 11-18.

DIRECTIONS: Questions 11 through 18 are to be answered SOLELY on the basis of the following information.

Below are listed the code number, name, and area of investigation of six detective units. Each question describes a crime.
For each question, choose the option (A, B, C, or D) which contains the code number for the detective unit responsible for handling that crime.

DETECTIVE UNITS

Unit Code No.	Unit Name	Unit's Area of Investigation
01	Senior Citizens Unit	All robberies of senior citizens 65 years or older
02	Major Case Unit	Any bank robbery; a commercial robbery where value of goods or money stolen is over $25,000
03	Robbery Unit	Any commercial, non-bank robbery where the value of the stolen goods or money is $25,000 or less; robberies of individuals under 65 years of age
04	Fraud and Larceny Unit	Confidence games and pickpockets
05	Special Investigations Unit	Burglaries of premises where the value of goods removed or monies taken is $15,000 or less
06	Burglary Unit	Burglaries of premises where the value of goods removed or monies taken is over $15,000

11. Mrs. Green calls the precinct and reports that her apartment was burglarized while she was on vacation and that precious jewelry and silverware, valued at $27,000, were taken.
    To which unit code number should her complaint be referred?
    A. 05   B. 02   C. 03   D. 06

12. Sylvia Bailey, Manager of the Building and Loan Savings Bank, reports that a man handed one of her tellers a note stating, *This is a robbery*. He had a gun and demanded money. The teller gave the man $500 in small bills, and the man then left.
    To which unit code should the complaint be referred?
    A. 02   B. 06   C. 03   D. 05

4 (#1)

13. Mrs. Miniver, a 67-year-old widow, states that she was beaten and robbed by two men in the elevator of her apartment building.
    To which unit code number should the complaint be referred?
    A. 06   B. 01   C. 03   D. 02

    13._____

14. Mr. Whipple, Manager of T.V.A. Supermarket, reports that during the night someone entered the store and removed merchandise valued at $12,500.
    To which unit code number should the complaint be referred?
    A. 05   B. 03   C. 06   D. 02

    14._____

15. Mr. Gold, owner of Gold's Jewelry Exchange, reports that two men, armed with shotguns, robbed his store and removed money and jewelry valued at $28,000.
    To which unit code number should the complaint be referred?
    A. 05   B. 03   C. 06   D. 02

    15._____

16. Mr. Watson, a 62-year-old man, was walking in Central Park when he was approached by a man with a knife and was robbed of $72.
    To which unit code number should the complaint be referred?
    A. 01   B. 06   C. 03   D. 02

    16._____

17. The Ace Jewelry Manufacturing Company was broken into over the weekend when the building was closed. The owner stated that $35,000 in gold, silver, diamonds, and jewelry were taken.
    To which unit code number should the complaint be referred?
    A. 02   B. 03   C. 06   D. 05

    17._____

18. Mrs. Vargas, 62, reports that she gave Mr. Greene of the Starlite Realty Corporation $1,000 to locate a new apartment for her family. A week went by, and she never heard from Mr. Greene. She called the Starlite Realty Corporation, and they informed her that Mr. Greene never worked for Starlite Realty Corporation and that they have no record of the $1,000 deposit of Mrs. Vargas.
    To which unit code number should the complaint be referred?
    A. 04   B. 03   C. 01   D. 05

    18._____

Questions 19-24.

DIRECTIONS: Questions 19 through 24 consist of sentences which contain examples of correct or incorrect English usage. Examine each sentence with reference to grammar, spelling, punctuation, and capitalization. Choose one of the following options that would be BEST for correct English usage:
A. The sentence is correct.
B. There is one mistake.
C. There are two mistakes.
D. There are three mistakes.

19. Mrs. Fitzgerald came to the 59th Precinct to retreive her property which were stolen earlier in the week.

    19._____

20. The two officer's responded to the call, only to find that the perpatrator and the   20._____
    victim have left the scene.

21. Mr. Coleman called the 61st Precinct to report that, upon arriving at his store,   21._____
    he discovered that there was a large hole in the wall and that three boxes of
    radios were missing

22. The Administrative Leiutenant of the 62nd Precinct held a meeting which was   22._____
    attended by all the civilians, assigned to the Precinct.

23. Three days after the robbery occured the detective apprahended two   23._____
    suspects and recovered the stolen items.

24. The Community Affairs Officer of the 64th Precinct is the liaison between   24._____
    the Precinct and the community; he works closely with various community
    organizations, and elected officials.

Questions 25-32.

DIRECTIONS: Questions 25 through 32 are to be answered on the basis of the following
paragraph, which contains some deliberate errors in spelling and/or grammar
and/or punctuation. Each line of the paragraph is preceded by a number.
There are 9 lines and 9 numbers.

Line No.	Paragraph Line
1	The protection of life and property are, one of
2	the oldest and most important functions of a city.
3	New York city has its own full-time police Agency.
4	The police Department has the power an it shall
5	be there duty to preserve the Public piece,
6	prevent crime detect and arrest offenders, suppress
7	riots, protect the rites of persons and property, etc.
8	The maintainance of sound relations with the community they
9	serve is an important function of law enforcement officers.

25. How many errors are contained in line one?   25._____
    A. One   B. Two   C. Three   D. None

26. How many errors are contained in line two?   26._____
    A. One   B. Two   C. Three   D. None

27. How many errors are contained in line three?   27._____
    A. One   B. Two   C. Three   D. None

28. How many errors are contained in line four?   28._____
    A. One   B. Two   C. Three   D. None

29. How many errors are contained in line five?
    A. One   B. Two   C. Three   D. None

    29._____

30. How many errors are contained in line six?
    A. One   B. Two   C. Three   D. None

    30._____

31. How many errors are contained in line seven?
    A. One   B. Two   C. Three   D. None

    31._____

32. How many errors are contained in line eight?
    A. One   B. Two   C. Three   D. None

    32._____

Questions 33-40.

DIRECTIONS: Questions 33 through 40 are to be answered on the basis of the material contained in the INDEX OF CRIME IN CENTRAL CITY, U.S.A. 2011-2020 appearing below. Certain information is various columns is deliberately left blank.
The correct answer (A, B, C, or D) to these questions requires you to make computations that will enable you to fill in the blanks correctly.

	INDEX OF CRIME IN CENTRAL CITY, U.S.A., 2011-2020								
	Crime Index Total	Violent Crime[1]	Property Crime[2]	Murder	Forcible Rape	Robbery	Aggravated Assault	Burglary	Larceny Theft	Motor Vehicle Theft
2011	8,717	875		19	51	385	420	2,565	4,347	930
2012	10,252	974	9278	20	55	443	456		5,262	977
2013	11,256	1,026	10,230	20		465	485	3,253	5,977	1,000
2014	11,304	986		18	58	420	490	3,089	6,270	959
2015	10,935	1,009	9,926	19	63	405	522	3,053	5,605	968
2016	11,140	1,061	10,079	19	67	417	558	3,104	5,983	992
2017	12,152	1,178	10,974	23	75	466	614	3,299	6,578	1,097
2018	13,294	1,308	11,986	23	83		654	3,759	7,113	1,114
2019	13,289	1,321	11,968	22	82	574	643	3,740	7,154	1,074
2020	12,856	1,285	11,571	22	77	536	650	3,415	7,108	1,048

33. What was the TOTAL number of Property Crimes in 2011?
    A. 9,740   B. 10,252   C. 16,559   D. 7,842

    33._____

34. What was the TOTAL number of Burglaries for 2012?
    A. 2,062   B. 3,039   C. 3,259   D. 4,001

    34._____

35. In 2020, the total number of Aggravated Assaults was MOST NEARLY what percent of the total number of Violent Crimes for that year?
    A. 49.1   B. 46.3   C. 50.6   D. 41.7

    35._____

36. In 2015, Property Crime was MOST NEARLY what percent of the Crime Index Total?
    A. 90.8   B. 9.3   C. 10.1   D. 89.9

    36._____

37. What was the TOTAL number of Property Crimes for 2014? 37._____
   A. 10,318   B. 11,304   C. 98   D. 10,808

38. What was the TOTAL number of Robberies for 2018? 38._____
   A. 654   B. 571   C. 548   D. 1,202

39. Robbery made up what percent of the TOTAL number of Violent Crimes for 2020? 39._____
   A. 68.8%   B. 4.1%   C. 21.9%   D. 41.7%

40. What was the TOTAL number of Forcible Rapes for 2013? 40._____
   A. 47   B. 56   C. 55   D. 101

KEY (CORRECT ANSWERS)

1.	D	11.	D	21.	A	31.	A
2.	B	12.	A	22.	C	32.	A
3.	B	13.	B	23.	C	33.	D
4.	A	14.	A	24.	B	34.	B
5.	D	15.	D	25.	C	35.	C
6.	D	16.	C	26.	D	36.	A
7.	B	17.	C	27.	C	37.	A
8.	C	18.	A	28.	B	38.	C
9.	D	19.	C	29.	C	39.	D
10.	D	20.	D	30.	B	40.	B

TEST 2

DIRECTIONS: Each question or incomplete statement is followed by several suggested answers or completions. Select the one that BEST answers the question or completes the statement. *PRINT THE LETTER OF THE CORRECT ANSWER IN THE SPACE AT THE RIGHT.*

Questions 1-8.

DIRECTIONS: Each of Questions 1 through 8 consists of three lines of code letters and numbers. The numbers on each line should correspond to the code letters on the same line in accordance with the table below.

Code Letter	X	B	L	T	V	M	P	F	J	S
Corresponding Number	0	1	2	3	4	5	6	7	8	9

On some of the lines, an error exists in the coding. Compare the letters and numbers in each question carefully. If you find an error or errors on:
Only <u>one</u> of the lines in the question, mark your answer A;
Any <u>two</u> of the lines in the question, mark your answer B;
All <u>three</u> lines in the question, mark your answer C;
<u>None</u> of the lines in the question, mark your answer D.

SAMPLE QUESTION: MSXVLPT—5904263
SBFJLTP—9178246
XVMBTPF—8451367

In the above sample, the first line is correct since each code letter listed has the correct corresponding number. On the second line, an error exists because code letter T should have number 3 instead of number 4. On the third line, an error exists because the code letter X should have the number 0 instead of the number 8. Since there are errors on two of the three lines, the correct answer is B.

1. VFSTPLM—4793625
   SBXFLTP—9017236
   BT[JFSV—1358794

2. TSLFVPJ—3927468
   JLFTVXS—8273409
   MVSXBFL—5490172

3. XFTJSVT—0739843
   VFMTFLB—4753721
   LTFJSFM—2378985

4. SJMSJVL—9859742
   VFBXMPF—3710568
   PFPXLBS—7670219

5. MFPXVFP—5764076　　　　　　　　　　　　　　　　　　　　　　　　　　　5.____
   PTFJBLX—6378120
   VXSVSTB—4094931

6. BXFPVJT—1076483　　　　　　　　　　　　　　　　　　　　　　　　　　　6.____
   STFMVLT—9375423
   TXPBTTM—3061335

7. VLSBLVP—4290246　　　　　　　　　　　　　　　　　　　　　　　　　　　7.____
   FPSFBMV—7679154
   XTMXMLL—0730522

8. JFVPMTJ—8746538　　　　　　　　　　　　　　　　　　　　　　　　　　　8.____
   TFPMXBL—3765012
   TJSFMFX—4987570

Questions 9-18.

DIRECTIONS: Questions 9 through 18 each consists of two columns, each containing four lines of names, numbers and/or addresses. For each question, compare the lines in Column I with the lines in Column II to see if they match exactly, and mark your answer (A, B, C, or D) according to the following instructions:
- A. all four lines match exactly
- B. only three lines match exactly
- C. only two lines match exactly
- D. only one line matches exactly

9. (1) Earl Hodgson　　　　　　　　　Earl Hodgson　　　　　　　　　　　9.____
    (2) 1409870　　　　　　　　　　　　1408970
    (3) Shore Ave.　　　　　　　　　　Schore Ave.
    (4) Macon Rd.　　　　　　　　　　 Macon Rd.

10. (1) 9671485　　　　　　　　　　　　9671485　　　　　　　　　　　　　10.____
    (2) 470 Astor Court　　　　　　　 470 Astor Court
    (3) Halprin, Phillip　　　　　　　Halperin, Phillip
    (4) Frank D. Poliseo　　　　　　　Frank D. Poliseo

11. (1) Tandem Associates　　　　　　 Tandom Associates　　　　　　　　11.____
    (2) 144-17 Northern Blvd.　　　　 144-17 Northern Blvd.
    (3) Alberta Forchi　　　　　　　　 Albert Forchi
    (4) Kings Park, NY 10751　　　　　Kings Point, NY 10751

12. (1) Bertha C. McCormack　　　　　 Bertha C. McCormack　　　　　　　12.____
    (2) Clayton, MO　　　　　　　　　　Clayton, MO
    (3) 976-4242　　　　　　　　　　　 976-4242
    (4) New City, NY 10951　　　　　　New City, NY 10951

3 (#2)

13. (1) George C. Morill   George C. Morrill   13._____
    (2) Columbia, SC 29201   Columbia, SD 29201
    (3) Louis Ingham   Louis Ingham
    (4) 3406 Forest Ave.   3406 Forest Ave.

14. (1) 506 S. Elliott Pl.   506 S. Elliott Pl.   14._____
    (2) Herbert Hall   Hurbert Hall
    (3) 4712 Rockaway Pkway   4712 Rockaway Pkway
    (4) 169 E. 7 St.   169 E. 7 St.

15. (1) 345 Park Ave.   345 Park Pl.   15._____
    (2) Colman Oven Corp.   Coleman Oven Corp.
    (3) Robert Conte   Robert Conti
    (4) 6179846   6179846

16. (1) Grigori Schierber   Grigori Schierber   16._____
    (2) Des Moines, Iowa   Des Moines, Iowa
    (3) Gouverneur Hospital   Gouverneur Hospital
    (4) 91-35 Cresskill Pl.   91-35 Cresskill Pl.

17. (1) Jeffery Janssen   Jeffrey Janssen   17._____
    (2) 8041071   8041071
    (3) 40 Rockefeller Plaza   40 Rockafeller Plaza
    (4) 407 6 St.   406 7 St.

18. (1) 5971996   5871996   18._____
    (2) 3113 Knickerbocker Ave.   3113 Knickerbocker Ave.
    (3) 8434 Boston Post Rd.   8424 Boston Post Rd.
    (4) Penn Station   Penn Station

Questions 19-22.

DIRECTIONS: Questions 19 through 22 are to be answered by looking at the 4 groups of names and addresses listed below (I, II, III, and IV) and then finding out the number of groups that have their corresponding numbered lines exactly the same.

Group I
Line 1 Ingersoll Public Library
Line 2 Reference and Research Dept.
Line 3 95-12 238 St.
Line 4 East Elmhurst, N.Y. 11357

Group II
Ingersoil Public Library
Reference and Research Dept.
95-12 238 St.
East Elmhurst, N.Y. 11357

Group III
Line 1 Ingersoll Public Library
Line 2 Reference and Research Dept.
Line 3 92-15 283 St.
Line 4 East Elmhurst, N.Y. 11357

Group IV
Ingersoll Poblic Library
Referance and Research Dept.
95-12 283 St.
East Elmhurst, N.Y. 1357

19. In how many groups is line one exactly the same? 19.____
    A. Two   B. Three   C. Four   D. None

20. In how many groups is line two exactly the same? 20.____
    A. Two   B. Three   C. Four   D. None

21. In how many groups is line three exactly the same? 20.____
    A. Two   B. Three   C. Four   D. None

22. In how many groups is line four exactly the same? 22.____
    A. Two   B. Three   C. Four   E. None

Questions 23-26.

DIRECTIONS: Questions 23 through 26 are to be answered by looking at the 4 groups of names and addresses listed below (I, II, III, and IV) and then finding out the number of groups that have their corresponding numbered lines exactly the same.

Group I
Line 1 Richmond General Hospital
Line 2 Geriatric Clinic
Line 3 3975 Paerdegat St.
Line 4 Loudonville, New York 11538

Group II
Richman General Hospital
Geriatric Clinic
3975 Peardegat St.
Londonville, New York 11538

Group III
Line 1 Richmond General Hospital
Line 2 Geriatric Clinic
Line 3 3795 Paerdegat St.
Line 4 Loudonville, New York 11358

Group IV
Richmend General Hospital
Geriatric Clinic
3975 Paerdegat St.
Loudonville, New York 11538

23. In how many groups is line one exactly the same? 23.____
    A. Two   B. Three   C. Four   D. None

24. In how many groups is line two exactly the same? 24.____
    A. Two   B. Three   C. Four   D. None

25. In how many groups is line three exactly the same? 25.____
    A. Two   B. Three   C. Four   D. None

26. In how many groups is line four exactly the same? 26.____
    A. Two   B. Three   C. Four   D. None

Questions 27-34.

DIRECTIONS: Each of Questions 27 through 34 consists of four or six numbered names. For each question, choose the option (A, B, C, or D) which indicates the order in which the names should be filed in accordance with the following file instructions:

5 (#2)

- File alphabetically according to last name, then first name, then middle initial.
- File according to each successive letter within a name.
- When comparing two names where the letters in the longer name are identical with the corresponding letters in the shorter name, the shorter name is filed first.
- When the last names are the same, initials are always filed before names beginning with the same letter.

27. I. Ralph Robinson
    II. Alfred Ross
    III. Luis Robles
    IV. James Roberts
    The CORRECT filing sequence for the above names should be
       A. IV, II, I, III   B. I, IV, III, II   C. III, IV, I, II   D. IV, I, III, II

28. I. Irwin Goodwin
    II. Inez Gonzalez
    III. Irene Goodman
    IV. Ira S. Goodwin
    V. Ruth I. Goldstein
    VI. M.B. Goodman
    The CORRECT filing sequence for the above names should be
       A. V, II, I, IV, III, VI   B. V, II, VI, III, IV, I
       C. V, II, III, VI, IV, I   D. V, II, III, VI, I, IV

29. I. George Allan
    II. Gregory Allen
    III. Gary Allen
    IV. George Allen
    The CORRECT filing sequence for the above names should be
       A. IV, III, I, II   B. I, IV, II, III   C. III, IV, I, II   D. I, III, IV, II

30. I. Simon Kauffman
    II. Leo Kauffman
    III. Robert Kaufmann
    IV. Paul Kauffman
    The CORRECT filing sequence for the above names should be
       A. I, IV, II, III   B. II, IV, I, III   C. III, II, IV, I   D. I, II, III, IV

31. I. Roberta Williams
    II. Robin Wilson
    III. Roberta Wilson
    IV. Robin Williams
    The CORRECT filing sequence for the above names should be
       A. III, II, IV, I   B. I, IV, III, II   C. I, II, III, IV   D. III, I, II, IV

27._____
28._____
29._____
30._____
31._____

6 (#2)

32. I.   Lawrence Shultz
     II. Albert Schultz
     III. Theodore Schwartz
     IV. Thomas Schwarz
     V.   Alvin Schultz
     VI. Leonard Shultz
     The CORRECT filing sequence for the above names should be
        A. II, V, III, IV, I, VI   B. IV, III, V, I, II, VI
        C. II, V, I, VI, III, IV   D. I, VI, II, V, III, IV

33. I.   McArdle
     II. Mayer
     III. Maletz
     IV. McNiff
     V.   Meyer
     VI. MacMahon
     The CORRECT filing sequence for the above names should be
        A. I, IV, VI, III, II, V   B. II, I, IV, VI, III, V
        C. VI, III, II, I, IV, V   D. VI, III, II, V, I, IV

34. I.   Jack E. Johnson
     II. R.H. Jackson
     III. Bertha Jackson
     IV. J.T. Johnson
     V.   Ann Johns
     VI. John Jacobs
     The CORRECT filing sequence for the above names should be
        A. II, III, VI, V, IV, I   B. III, II, VI, V, IV, I
        C. VI, II, III, I, V, IV   D. III, II, VI, IV, V, I

Questions 35-40.

DIRECTIONS: Questions 35 through 40 are to be answered SOLELY on the basis of the following passage.

An aide assigned to the Complaint Room must be familiar with the various forms used by that office. Some of these forms and their uses are:

Form	Use
Complaint Report:	Used to record information on or information about crimes reported to the Police Department.
Complaint Report Follow-Up:	Used to record additional information after the initial complaint report has been filed
Aided Card:	Used to record information pertaining to sick and injured persons aided by the police.
Accident Report:	Used to record information on or information about injuries and/or property damage involving motorized vehicles.
Property Vouch:	Used to record information on or information about property which comes into possession of the Police Department. (Motorized vehicles are not included.)

Auto Voucher: Used to record information on or information about a motorized vehicle which comes into possession of the Police Department.

35. Mr. Brown walks into the police precinct and informs the Administrative Aide that, while he was at work, someone broke into his apartment and removed property belonging to him. He does not know everything that was taken, but he wants to make a report now and will make a list of what was taken and bring it in later.
According to the above passage, the CORRECT form to use in this situation should be the
   A. Property Voucher
   B. Complaint Report
   C. Complaint Report Follow-Up
   D. Aided Card

36. Mrs. Wilson telephones the precinct and informs the Administrative Aide she wishes to report additional property which was taken from her apartment. The Administrative Aide finds a Complaint Report had been previously filed for Mrs. Wilson.
According to the above passage, the CORRECT form to use in this situation should be the
   A. Property Voucher
   B. Complaint Report
   C. Complaint Report Follow-Up
   D. Aided Card

37. Police Officer Jones walks into the Complaint Room and informs the Administrative Aide that, while he was on patrol, he observed a woman fall to the sidewalk and remain there, apparently hurt. He comforted the injured woman and called for an ambulance, which came and brought the woman to the hospital.
According to the above passage, the CORRECT form on which to record this information should be the
   A. Accident Report
   B. Complaint Report
   C. Complaint Report Follow-Up
   D. Aided Card

38. Police Officer Smith informed the Administrative Aide assigned to the Complaint Room that Mr. Green, while crossing the street, was struck by a motorcycle and had to be taken to the hospital.
According to the above passage, the facts regarding this incident should be recorded on which one of the following forms?
   A. Accident Report
   B. Complaint Report
   C. Complaint Report Follow-Up
   D. Aided Card

39. Police Officer Williams reports to the Administrative Aide assigned to the Complaint Room that he and his partner, Police Officer Murphy, found an auto which was reported stolen and had the auto towed into the police garage.
Of the following forms listed in the above passage, which is the CORRECT one to use to record this information?
   A. Property Voucher
   B. Auto Voucher
   C. Complaint Report Follow-Up
   D. Complaint Report

40. Administrative Aide Lopez has been assigned to the Complaint Room. During her tour of duty, a person who does not identify herself hands Ms. Lopez a purse. The person states that she found the purse on the street. She then leaves the station house.
According to the information in the above passage, which is the CORRECT form to fill out to record the incident?
    A. Property Voucher
    B. Auto Voucher
    C. Complaint Report Follow-Up
    D. Complaint Report

40._____

KEY (CORRECT ANSWERS)

1.	B	11.	D	21.	A	31.	B
2.	D	12.	A	22.	C	32.	A
3.	B	13.	C	23.	A	33.	C
4.	C	14.	B	24.	C	34.	B
5.	A	15.	D	25.	A	35.	B
6.	D	16.	A	26.	A	36.	C
7.	C	17.	D	27.	D	37.	D
8.	A	18.	C	28.	C	38.	A
9.	C	19.	A	29.	D	39.	B
10.	B	20.	B	30.	B	40.	A

NAME AND NUMBER CHECKING
EXAMINATION SECTION
TEST 1

DIRECTIONS: This test is designed to measure your speed/and accuracy. You are urged to work both quickly and accurately and to do correctly as many lists as you can in the time allowed. The test consists of lists or pairs of names and numbers. Count the number of IDENTICAL pairs in each list. Then, select the correct number, 1, 2, 3, 4, 5, and indicate your choice in the space at the right. Two sample questions are presented for your guidance, together with the correct solutions.

SAMPLE LIST A
Adelphi College — Adelphia College
Braxton Corp — Braxeton Corp.
Wassaic State School — Wassaic State School
Central Islip State Hospital — Central Isllip State Hospital
Greenwich House — Greenwich House

NOTE: There are only two correct pairs—Wassaic State School and Greenwich House. Therefore, the CORRECT answer is 2.

SAMPLE LIST B
78453694 — 78453684
784530 — 784530
533 — 534
67845 — 67845
2368745 — 2368755

NOTE: There are only two correct pairs—784530 and 67845. Therefore, the CORRECT answer is 2.

LIST 1   1.____
   98654327 - 98654327
   74932564 - 7492564
   61438652 - 61438652
   01297653 - 01287653
   1865439765 - 1865439765

LIST 2   2.____
   478362 - 478363
   278354792 - 278354772
   9327 - 9327
   297384625 - 27384625
   6428156 - 6428158

2 (#1)

LIST 3
    Abbey House   - Abbey House
    Actor's Fund Home   - Actor's Fund Home
    Adrian Memorial   - Adrian Memorial
    A. Clayton Powell Home   - Clayton Powell House
    Abbot E. Kittredge Club   - Abbott E. Kitteredge Club

3.____

LIST 4
    3682   - 3692
    21937453829   - 31927453829
    723   - 733
    2763920   - 2763920
    47293   - 47293

4.____

LIST 5
    Adra House   - Adra House
    Adolescents' Court   - Adolescents' Court
    Cliff Villa   - Cliff Villa
    Clark Neighborhood House   - Clark Neighborhood House
    Alma Mathews House   - Alma Mathews House

5.____

LIST 6
    28734291   - 28734271
    63810263849   - 63810263846
    26831027   - 26831027
    368291   - 368291
    7238102637   - 7238102637

6.____

LIST 7
    Albion State T.S.   - Albion State T.C.
    Clara de Hirsch Home   - Clara De Hirsch Home
    Alice Carrington Royce   - Alice Carington Royce
    Alice Chopin Nursery   - Alice Chapin Nursery
    Lighthouse Eye Clinic   - Lighthouse Eye Clinic

7.____

LIST 8
    327   - 329
    712438291026   - 712438291026
    2753829142   - 275382942
    826287   - 826289
    26435162839   - 26435162839

8.____

LIST 9
    Letchworth Village   - Letchworth Village
    A.A.A.E. Inc.   - A.A.A.E. Inc.
    Clear Pool Camp   - Clear Pool Camp
    A.M.M.L.A. Inc.   - A.M.M.L.A. Inc.
    J.G. Harbard   - J.G. Harbord

9.____

3 (#1)

LIST 10
    8254   - 8256
    2641526   - 2641526
    4126389012   - 4126389102
    725   - 725
    76253917287   - 76253917287

10.____

LIST 11
    Attica State Prison   - Attica State Prison
    Nellie Murrah   - Nellie Murrah
    Club Marshall   - Club Marshal
    Assissium Casea-Maria - Assissium Casa-Maria
    The Homestead   - The Homestead

11.____

LIST 12
    2691   - 2691
    623819253627   - 623819253629
    28637   - 28937
    278392736   - 278392736
    52739   - 52739

12.____

LIST 13
    A.I.C.P. Boys Camp   - A.I.C.P. Boy's Camp
    Einar Chrystie   - Einar Christyie
    Astoria Center   - Astoria Center
    G. Frederick Brown   - G. Federick Browne
    Vacation Service   - Vacation Services

13.____

LIST 14
    728352689   - 728352688
    643728   - 643728
    37829176   - 37827196
    8425367   - 8425369
    65382018   - 65382018

14.____

LIST 15
    E.S. Streim   - E.S. Strim
    Charles E. Higgins   - Charles E. Higgins
    Baluvelt, N.Y.   - Blauwelt, N.Y.
    Roberta Magdalen   - Roberto Magdalen
    Ballard School   - Ballard School

15.____

LIST 16
    7382   - 7392
    281374538299   - 291374538299
    623   - 633
    6273730   - 6273730
    63392   - 63392

16.____

LIST 17
Orrin Otis — - Orrin Otis
Barat Settlement — - Barat Settlemen
Emmanuel House — - Emmanuel House
William T. McCreery — - William T. McCreery
Seamen's Home — - Seaman's Home

17.____

LIST 18
72824391 — - 72834371
3729106237 — - 37291106237
82620163849 — - 82620163846
37638921 — - 37638921
82631027 — - 82631027

18.____

LIST 19
Commonwealth Fund — - Commonwealth Fund
Anne Johnsen — - Anne Johnson
Bide-A-Wee Home — - Bide-a-Wee Home
Riverdale-on-Hudson — - Riverdal-on-Hudson
Bialystoker Home — - Bailystoker Home

19.____

LIST 20
9271 — - 9271
392918352627 — - 392018852629
72637 — - 72637
927392736 — - 927392736
92739 — - 92739

20.____

LIST 21
Charles M. Stump — - Charles M. Stump
Bourne Workshop — - Buorne Workshop
B'nai Bi'rith — - B'nai Brith
Poppenhuesen Institute — - Poppenheusen Institute
Consular Service — - Consular Service

21.____

LIST 22
927352689 — - 927352688
647382 — - 648382
93729176 — - 93727196
649536718 — - 649536718
5835367 — - 5835369

22.____

LIST 23
L.S. Bestend — - L.S. Bestent
Hirsch Mfg. Co. — - Hircsh Mfg. Co.
F.H. Storrs — - F.P. Storrs
Camp Wassaic — - Camp Wassaic
George Ballingham — - George Ballingham

23.____

LIST 24
- 372846392048 — - 372846392048
- 334 — - 334
- 7283524678 — - 7283524678
- 7283 — - 7283
- 7283629372 — - 7283629372

24.____

LIST 25
- Dr. Stiles Company — - Dr. Stills Company
- Frances Hunsdon — - Frances Hunsdon
- Northrop Barrert — - Nothrup Barrent
- J.D. Brunjes — - J.D. Brunjes
- Theo. Claudel & Co. — - Theo. Claudel co.

25.____

KEY (CORRECT ANSWERS)

1.	3		11.	3
2.	1		12.	3
3.	2		13.	1
4.	2		14.	2
5.	5		15.	2
6.	3		16.	2
7.	1		17.	3
8.	2		18.	2
9.	4		19.	2
10.	3		20.	4

21. 2
22. 1
23. 2
24. 5
25. 2

TEST 2

DIRECTIONS: This test is designed to measure your speed/and accuracy. You are urged to work both quickly and accurately and to do correctly as many lists as you can in the time allowed. The test consists of lists or pairs of names and numbers. Count the number of IDENTICAL pairs in each list. Then, select the correct number, 1, 2, 3, 4, 5, and indicate your choice in the space at the right.

LIST 1
    82728   - 82738
    82736292637   - 82736292639
    728   - 738
    83926192527   - 83726192529
    82736272   - 82736272

1.____

LIST 2
    L. Pietri   - L. Pietri
    Mathewson, L.F.   - Mathewson, L.F.
    Funk & Wagnall   - Funk & Wagnalls
    Shimizu, Sojio   - Shimizu, Sojio
    Filing Equipment Bureau - Filing Equipment Buraeu

2.____

LIST 3
    63801829374   - 63801839474
    283577657   - 283577657
    65689   - 65689
    3457892026   - 3547893026
    2779   - 2778

3.____

LIST 4
    August Caille   - August Caille
    The Well-Fare Service   - The Wel-Fare Service
    K.L.M. Process co.   - R.L.M. Process Co.
    Merrill Littell   - Merrill Littell
    Dodd & Sons   - Dodd & Son

4.____

LIST 5
    998745732   - 998745733
    723   - 723
    463849102983   - 463849102983
    8570   - 8570
    279012   - 279012

5.____

LIST 6
    M.A. Wender   - M.A. Winder
    Minneapolis Supply Co. - Minneapolis Supply Co.
    Beverly Hills Corp   - Beverley Hills Corp.
    Trafalgar Square   - Trafalgar Square
    Phifer, D.T.   - Phiefer, D.T.

6.____

2 (#2)

LIST 7   7.____
    7834629   - 7834629
    3549806746   - 3549806746
    97802564   - 97892564
    689246   - 688246
    2578024683   - 2578024683

LIST 8   8.____
    Scadrons'   - Scadrons'
    Gensen & Bro.   - Genson & Bro.
    Firestone Co.   - Firestone Co.
    H.L. Eklund   - H.L. Eklund
    Oleomargarine Co.   - Oleomargarine Co.

LIST 9   9.____
    782039485618   - 782039485618
    53829172639   - 63829172639
    892   - 892
    82937482   - 829374820
    52937456   - 53937456

LIST 10   10.____
    First Nat'l Bank   - First Nat'l Bank
    Sedgwick Machine Works   - Sedgewick Machine Works
    Hectographia Co.   - Hectographia Corp.
    Levet Bros.   - Levet Bros.
    Multistamp Co., Inc.   - Multistamp Co., Inc.

LIST 11   11.____
    7293   - 7293
    6382910293   - 6382910292
    981928374012   - 981928374912
    58293   - 58393
    18203649271   - 283019283745

LIST 12   12.____
    Lowrey Lb'r Co.   - Lowrey Lb'r Co.
    Fidelity Service   - Fidelity Service
    Reumann, J.A.   - Reumann, J.A.
    Duophoto Ltd.   - Duophotos Ltd.
    John Jarratt   - John Jaratt

LIST 13   13.____
    6820384   - 6820384
    383019283745   - 383019283745
    63927102   - 63928102
    91029354829   - 91029354829
    58291728   - 58291728

LIST 14
- Standard Press Co.   - Standard Press Co.
- Reliant Mf'g. Co.   - Relant Mf'g Co.
- M.C. Lynn   - M.C. Lynn
- J. Fredericks Company   - G. Fredericks Company
- Wandermann, B.S.   - Wanderman, B.S.

14.____

LIST 15
- 4283910293   - 4283010203
- 992018273648   - 992018273848
- 620   - 629
- 752937273   - 752937373
- 5392   - 5392

15.____

LIST 16
- Waldorf Hotel   - Waldorf Hotel
- Aaron Machinery Co.   - Aaron Machinery Co.
- Caroline Ann Locke   - Caroline Ane Locke
- McCabe Mfg. Co.   - McCabe Mfg. Co.
- R.L. Landres   - R.L. Landers

16.____

LIST 17
- 68391028364   - 68391028394
- 68293   - 68293
- 739201   - 739201
- 72839201   - 72839211
- 739917   - 739719

17.____

LIST 18
- Balsam M.M.   - Balsamm, M.M.
- Steinway & Co.   - Stienway & M. Co.
- Eugene Elliott   - Eugene A. Elliott
- Leonard Loan Co.   - Leonard Loan Co.
- Frederick Morgan   - Frederick Morgen

18.____

LIST 19
- 8929   - 9820
- 392836472829   - 392836572829
- 462   - 4622039271
- 827   - 2039276837
- 53829   - 54829

19.____

LIST 20
- Danielson's Hofbrau   - Danielson's Hafbrau
- Edward A. Truarme   - Edward A. Truame
- Insulite Co.   - Insulite Co.
- Reisler Shoe Corp.   - Rielser Shoe Corp.
- L.L. Thompson   - L.L. Thompson

20.____

LIST 21
    92839102837
    58891028
    7291728
    272839102839
    428192

- 92839102837
- 58891028
- 7291928
- 272839102839
- 428102

21.____

LIST 22
    K.L. Veiller
    Webster, Roy
    Drasner Spring Co.
    Edward J. Cravenport
    Harold Field

- K.L. Veiller
- Webster, Ray
- Drasner Spring Co.
- Edward J. Cravanport
- Harold A. Field

22.____

LIST 23
    2293
    4283910293
    871928374012
    68293
    8120364927

- 2293
- 5382910292
- 871928374912
- 68393
- 81293649271

23.____

LIST 24
    Tappe, Inc
    A.M. Wentingworth
    Scott A. Elliott
    Echeverria Corp.
    Bradford Victor Company

- Tappe, Inc.
- A.M. Wentinworth
- Scott A. Elliott
- Echeverria Corp.
- Bradford Victer Company

24.____

LIST 25
    4820384
    393019283745
    63917102
    91029354829
    48291728

- 4820384
- 283919283745
- 63927102
- 91029354829
- 48291728

25.____

KEY (CORRECT ANSWERS)

1.	1	11.	1
2.	3	12.	3
3.	2	13.	4
4.	2	14.	2
5.	4	15.	1
6.	2	16.	3
7.	3	17.	2
8.	4	18.	1
9.	2	19.	1
10.	3	20.	2

21.	3
22.	2
23.	1
24.	2
25.	4

ARITHMETIC

EXAMINATION SECTION
TEST 1

DIRECTIONS: Each question or incomplete statement is followed by several suggested answers or completions. Select the one that BEST answers the question or completes the statement. *PRINT THE LETTER OF THE CORRECT ANSWER IN THE SPACE AT THE RIGHT.*

1. From 30983 subtract 29998. The answer should be
   A. 985   B. 995   C. 1005   D. 1015

2. From $2537.75 subtract $1764.28. The answer should be
   A. $763.58   B. $773.47   C. $774.48   D. $873.58

3. From 254211 subtract 76348. The answer should be
   A. 177863   B. 177963   C. 187963   D. 188973

4. Divide 4025 by 35. The answer should be
   A. 105   B. 109   C. 115   D. 125

5. Multiply 0.35 by 2764. The answer should be
   A. 997.50   B. 967.40   C. 957.40   D. 834.40

6. Multiply 1367 by 0.50. The answer should be
   A. 6.8350   B. 68.350   C. 683.50   D. 6835.0

7. Multiply 841 by 0.01. The answer should be
   A. 0.841   B. 8.41   C. 84.1   D. 841

8. Multiply 1962 by 25. The answer should be
   A. 47740   B. 48460   C. 48950   D. 49050

9. Multiply 905 by 0.05. The answer should be
   A. 452.5   B. 45.25   C. 4.525   D. 0.4525

10. Multiply 8.93 by 4.7. The answer should be
    A. 41.971   B. 40.871   C. 4.1971   D. 4.0871

11. Multiply 25 by 763. The answer should be
    A. 18075   B. 18875   C. 19075   D. 20965

12. Multiply 2530 by 0.10. The answer should be
    A. 2.5300   B. 25.300   C. 253.00   D. 2530.0

13. Multiply 3053 by 0.25. The answer should be   13.____
    A. 76.325   B. 86.315   C. 763.25   D. 863.15

14. Multiply 6204 by 0.35. The answer should be   14.____
    A. 2282.40   B. 2171.40   C. 228.24   D. 217.14

15. Multiply $.35 by 7619. The answer should be   15.____
    A. $2324.75   B. $2565.65   C. $2666.65   D. $2756.75

16. Multiply 6513 by 45. The answer should be   16.____
    A. 293185   B. 293085   C. 292185   D. 270975

17. Multiply 3579 by 70. The answer should be   17.____
    A. 25053.0   B. 240530   C. 250530   D. 259530

18. A class had an average of 24 words correct on a spelling test. The class average on this   18.____
    spelling test was 80%.
    The AVERAGE number of words missed on this test was
    A. 2   B. 4   C. 6   D. 8

19. In which one of the following is 24 renamed as a product of primes?   19.____
    A. 2 x 6 x 2   B. 8 x 3 x 1
    C. 2 x 2 x 3 x 2   D. 3 x 4 x 2

Questions 20-23.

   DIRECTIONS: In answering Questions 20 through 23, perform the indicated operation. Select the BEST answer from the choices below.

20. Add: 7068   20.____
            2807
            9434
            6179

    A. 26,488   B. 24,588   C. 25,488   D. 25,478

21. Divide: 75√45555   21.____

    A. 674   B. 607.4   C. 6074   D. 60.74

22. Multiply: 907   22.____
                x806

    A. 73,142   B. 13,202   C. 721,042   D. 731,042

23. Subtract: 60085   23.____
                -47194

    A. 12,891   B. 13,891   C. 12,991   D. 12,871

24. A librarian reported that 1/5% of all books taken out last school year had not been returned.
If 85,000 books were borrowed from the library, how many were not returned?

    A. 170   B. 425   C. 1,700   D. 4,250

24._____

25. At 40 miles per hour, how many minutes would it take to travel 12 miles?

    A. 30   B. 18   C. 15   D. 20

25._____

KEY (CORRECT ANSWERS)

1. A		11. C	
2. B		12. C	
3. A		13. C	
4. C		14. B	
5. B		15. C	
6. C		16. B	
7. B		17. C	
8. D		18. C	
9. B		19. C	
10. A		20. C	

    21. B
    22. D
    23. A
    24. A
    25. B

SOLUTIONS TO PROBLEMS

1. 30,983 - 29,998 = 985

2. $2537.75 - $1764.28 = $773.47

3. 254,211 - 76,348 = 177,863

4. 4025 ÷ 35 = 115

5. (.35)(2764) = 967.4

6. (1367)(.50) = 683.5

7. (841)(.01) = 8.41

8. (1962)(25) = 49,050

9. (905)(.05) = 45.25

10. (8.93)(4.7) = 41.971

11. (25)(763) = 19,075

12. (2530)(.10) = 253

13. (3053)(.25) = 763.25

14. (6204)(.35) = 2171.4

15. ($.35)(7619) = $2666.65

16. (6513)(45) = 293,085

17. (3579)(70) = 250,530

18. 24 ÷ .80 = 30. Then, 30 - 24 = 6 words

19. 24 = 2 x 2 x 3 x 2, where each number is a prime.

20. 7068 ÷ 2807 + 9434 + 6179 = 25,488

21. 45,555 ÷ 75 = 607.4

22. (907)(806) = 731,042

23. 60,085 - 47,194 = 12,891

24. (1/5%)(85,000) = (.002)(85,000) = 170 books

25. Let x = number of minutes. Then, $\frac{40}{60} = \frac{12}{x}$. Solving, x = 18

TEST 2

DIRECTIONS: Each question or incomplete statement is followed by several suggested answers or completions. Select the one that BEST answers the question or completes the statement. *PRINT THE LETTER OF THE CORRECT ANSWER IN THE SPACE AT THE RIGHT.*

1. The sum of 57901 + 34762 is 1.____
   A. 81663   B. 82663   C. 91663   D. 92663

2. The sum of 559 + 448 + 362 + 662 is 2.____
   A. 2121   B. 2031   C. 2021   D. 1931

3. The sum of 36153 + 28624 + 81379 is 3.____
   A. 136156   B. 146046   C. 146146   D. 146156

4. The sum of 742 + 9197 + 8972 is 4.____
   A. 19901   B. 18911   C. 18801   D. 17921

5. The sum of 7989 + 8759 + 2726 is 5.____
   A. 18455   B. 18475   C. 19464   D. 19474

6. The sum of $111.55 + $95.05 + $38.80 is 6.____
   A. $234.40   B. $235.30   C. $245.40   D. $254.50

7. The sum of 1302 + 46187 + 92610 + 4522 is 7.____
   A. 144621   B. 143511   C. 134621   D. 134521

8. The sum of 47953 + 58041 + 63022 + 22333 is 8.____
   A. 170248   B. 181349   C. 191349   D. 200359

9. The sum of 76563 + 43693 + 38521 + 50987 + 72723 is 9.____
   A. 271378   B. 282386   C. 282487   D. 292597

10. The sum of 85923 + 97211 + 11333 + 4412 + 22533 is 10.____
    A. 209302   B. 212422   C. 221412   D. 221533

11. The sum of 4299 + 54163 + 89765 + 1012 + 38962 is 11.____
    A. 188201   B. 188300   C. 188301   D. 189311

12. The sum of 48526 + 709 + 11534 + 80432 + 6096 is 12.____
    A. 135177   B. 139297   C. 147297   D. 149197

13. The sum of $407.62 + $109.01 + $68.44 + $378.68 is 13.____
    A. $963.75   B. $964.85   C. $973.65   D. $974.85

14. From 40614 subtract 4697. The answer should be   14._____
    A. 35917   B. 35927   C. 36023   D. 36027

15. From 81773 subtract 5717. The answer should be   15._____
    A. 75964   B. 76056   C. 76066   D. 76956

16. From $1755.35 subtract $1201.75. The answer should be   16._____
    A. $542.50   B. $544.50   C. $553.60   D. $554.60

17. From $2402.10 subtract $998.85. The answer should be   17._____
    A. $1514.35   B. $1504.25   C. $1413.25   D. $1403.25

18. Add: 12 1/2
            2 1/2
            3 1/2   18._____
    A. 17   B. 17 1/4   C. 17 3/4   D. 18

19. Subtract: 150
                -80   19._____
    A. 70   B. 80   C. 130   D. 150

20. After cleaning up some lots in the city dump, five cleanup crews loaded the following   20._____
    amounts of garbage on trucks:
        Crew No. 1 loaded 2 1/4 tons
        Crew No. 2 loaded 3 tons
        Crew No. 3 loaded 1 1/4 tons
        Crew No. 4 loaded 2 1/4 tons
        Crew No. 5 loaded 1/2 ton.
    The TOTAL number of tons of garbage loaded was
    A. 8 1/4   B. 8 3/4   C. 9   D. 9 1/4

21. Subtract: 17 3/4
                -7 1/4   21._____
    A. 7 1/2   B. 10 1/2   C. 14 1/4   D. 17 3/4

22. Yesterday, Tom and Bill each received 10 leaflets about rat control. They were supposed   22._____
    to distribute one leaflet to each supermarket in the neighborhood. When the day was
    over, Tom had 8 leaflets left. Bill had no leaflets left.
    How many supermarkets got leaflets yesterday?
    A. 8   B. 10   C. 12   D. 18

23. What is 2/3 of 1 1/8?   23._____
    A. 1 11/16   B. 3/4   C. 3/8   D. 4 1/3

24. A farmer bought a load of 120 bushels of corn.   24._____
    After he fed 45 bushels to his hogs, what fraction of his supply remained?
    A. 5/8   B. 3/5   C. 3/8   D. 4/7

25. In the numeral 3,159,217, the 2 is in the _____ column. 25._____

    A. hundreds   B. units   C. thousands   D. tens

KEY (CORRECT ANSWERS)

1.	D	11.	A
2.	B	12.	C
3.	D	13.	A
4.	B	14.	A
5.	D	15.	B
6.	C	16.	C
7.	A	17.	D
8.	C	18.	D
9.	C	19.	A
10.	C	20.	D

21. B
22. C
23. B
24. A
25. A

SOLUTIONS TO PROBLEMS

1. 57,901 + 34,762 = 92,663

2. 559 + 448 + 362 + 662 = 2031

3. 36,153 + 28,624 + 81,379 = 146,156

4. 742 + 9197 + 8972 = 18,911

5. 7989 + 8759 + 2726 = 19,474

6. $111.55 + $95.05 + $38.80 = $245.40

7. 1302 + 46,187 + 92,610 + 4522 = 144,621

8. 47,953 + 58,041 + 63,022 + 22,333 = 191,349

9. 76,563 + 45,693 + 38,521 + 50,987 + 72,723 = 282,487

10. 85,923 + 97,211 + 11,333 + 4412 + 22,533 = 221,412

11. 4299 + 54,163 + 89,765 + 1012 + 38,962 = 188,201

12. 48,526 + 709 + 11,534 + 80,432 + 6096 = 147,297

13. $407.62 + $109.01 + $68.44 + $378.68 = $963.75

14. 40,614 - 4697 = 35,917

15. 81,773 - 5717 = 76,056

16. $1755.35 - $1201.75 = $553.60

17. $2402.10 - $998.85 = $1403.25

18. 12 1/2 + 2 1/4 + 3 1/4 = 17 4/4 = 18

19. 150 - 80 = 70

20. 2 1/4 + 3 + 1 1/4 + 2 1/4 + 1/2 = 8 5/4 = 9 1/4 tons

21. 17 3/4 - 7 1/4 = 10 2/4 = 10 1/2

22. 10 + 10 - 8 - 0 = 12 supermarkets

23. $(\frac{2}{3})(1\frac{1}{8}) = (\frac{2}{3})(\frac{9}{8}) = \frac{18}{24} = \frac{3}{4}$

24. 120 - 45 = 75. Then, $\frac{75}{120} = \frac{5}{8}$

25. The number 2 is in the hundreds column of 3,159,217

TEST 3

DIRECTIONS: Each question or incomplete statement is followed by several suggested answers or completions. Select the one that BEST answers the question or completes the statement. *PRINT THE LETTER OF THE CORRECT ANSWER IN THE SPACE AT THE RIGHT.*

1. The distance covered in three minutes by a subway train traveling at 30 mph is _____ mile(s).   1._____

    A. 3   B. 2   C. 1 1/2   D. 1

2. A crate contains 3 pieces of equipment weighing 73, 84, and 47 pounds, respectively. The empty crate weighs 16 pounds.   2._____
   If the crate is lifted by 4 trackmen, each trackman lifting one corner of the crate, the AVERAGE number of pounds lifted by each of the trackmen is

    A. 68   B. 61   C. 55   D. 51

3. The weight per foot of a length of square-bar 4" x 4" in cross-section, as compared with one 2" x 2" in cross-section, is _____ as much.   3._____

    A. twice   B. 2 1/2 times
    C. 3 times   D. 4 times

4. An order for 360 feet of 2" x 8" lumber is shipped in 20-foot lengths.   4._____
   The MAXIMUM number of 9-foot pieces that can be cut from this shipment is

    A. 54   B. 40   C. 36   D. 18

5. If a trackman gets $10.40 per hour and time and one-half for working over 40 hours, his gross salary for a week in which he worked 44 hours should be   5._____

    A. $457.60   B. $478.40   C. $499.20   D. $514.80

6. If a section of ballast 6'-0" wide, 8'-0" long, and 2'-6" deep is excavated, the amount of ballast removed is _____ cu. feet.   6._____

    A. 96   B. 104   C. 120   D. 144

7. The sum of 7'2 3/4", 0'-2 7/8", 3'-0", 4'-6 3/8", and 1'-9 1/4" is   7._____

    A. 16'-8 1/4"   B. 16'-8 3/4"   C. 16'-9 1/4"   D. 16'-9 3/4"

8. The sum of 3 1/16", 4 1/4", 2 5/8", and 5 7/16" is   8._____

    A. 15 3/16"   B. 15 1/4"   C. 15 3/8"   D. 15 1/2"

9. Add: $51.79, $29.39, and $8.98.   9._____
   The CORRECT answer is

    A. $78.97   B. $88.96   C. $89.06   D. $90.16

10. Add: $72.07 and $31.54. Then subtract $25.75.   10._____
    The CORRECT answer is

    A. $77.86   B. $82.14   C. $88.96   D. $129.36

2 (#3)

11. Start with $82.47. Then subtract $25.50, $4.75, and 35¢. 11.____
 The CORRECT answer is

 A. $30.60   B. $51.87   C. $52.22   D. $65.25

12. Add: $19.35 and $37.75. Then subtract $9.90 and $19.80. 12.____
 The CORRECT answer is

 A. $27.40   B. $37.00   C. $37.30   D. $47.20

13. Add: $153 13.____
          114
          210
         +186

 A. $657   B. $663   C. $713   D. $757

14. Add: $64.91 14.____
          13.53
          19.27
          20.00
         +72.84

 A. $170.25   B. $178.35   C. $180.45   D. $190.55

15. Add: 1963 15.____
          1742
         +2497

 A. 6202   B. 6022   C. 5212   D. 5102

16. Add: 206 16.____
           709
          1342
         +2076

 A. 3432   B. 3443   C. 4312   D. 4333

17. Subtract: $190.76 17.____
              -   .99

 A. $189.97   B. $189.87   C. $189.77   D. $189.67

18. From 99876 subtract 85397. The answer should be 18.____
 A. 14589   B. 14521   C. 14479   D. 13589

19. From $876.51 subtract $92.89. The answer should be 19.____
 A. $773.52   B. $774.72   C. $783.62   D. $784.72

20. From 70935 subtract 49489. The answer should be 20.____
 A. 20436   B. 21446   C. 21536   D. 21546

100

21. From $391.55 subtract $273.45. The answer should be 21._____
    A. $118.10   B. $128.20   C. $178.10   D. $218.20

22. When 119 is subtracted from the sum of 2016 + 1634, the answer is 22._____
    A. 2460   B. 3531   C. 3650   D. 3769

23. Multiply 35 x 65 x 15. The answer should be 23._____
    A. 2275   B. 24265   C. 31145   D. 34125

24. Multiply: 4.06 24._____
              x.031
    A. 1.2586   B. .12586   C. .02586   D. .1786

25. When 65 is added to the result of 14 multiplied by 13, the answer is 25._____
    A. 92   B. 182   C. 247   D. 16055

KEY (CORRECT ANSWERS)

1.	C	11.	B
2.	C	12.	A
3.	D	13.	B
4.	C	14.	D
5.	B	15.	A
6.	C	16.	D
7.	C	17.	C
8.	C	18.	C
9.	D	19.	C
10.	A	20.	B

21. A
22. B
23. D
24. B
25. C

SOLUTIONS TO PROBLEMS

1. Let x = distance. Then, $\dfrac{30}{60} = \dfrac{x}{3}$ Solving, x = 1 1/2 miles

2. (73 + 84 + 47 + 16) ÷ 4 = 55 pounds

3. (4 x 4) ÷ (2 x 2) = a ratio of 4 to 1.

4. 20 ÷ 9 = 2 2/9, rounded down to 2 pieces. Then, (360 ÷ 20)(2) = 36

5. Salary = ($10.40)(40) + ($15.60)(4) = $478.40

6. (6)(8)(2 1/2) = 120 cu.ft.

7. $7'2\dfrac{3}{4}" + 0'2\dfrac{7}{8}" + 3'0" + 4'6\dfrac{3}{8}" + 1'9\dfrac{1}{4}" = 15'19\dfrac{18}{8}" = 15'21\dfrac{1}{4}" = 16'9\dfrac{1}{4}"$

8. $3\dfrac{1}{16}" + 4\dfrac{1}{4}" + 2\dfrac{5}{8}" + 5\dfrac{7}{16}" = 14\dfrac{22}{16}" = 15\dfrac{3}{8}"$

9. $51.79 + $29.39 + $8.98 = $90.16

10. $72.07 + $31.54 = $103.61. Then, $103.61 - $25.75 = $77.86

11. $82.47 - $25.50 - $4.75 - $0.35 = $51.87

12. $19.35 + $37.75 = $57.10. Then, $57.10 - $9.90 - $19.80 = $27.40

13. $153 + $114 + $210 + $186 = $663

14. $64.91 + $13.53 + $19.27 + $20.00 + $72.84 = $190.55

15. 1963 + 1742 + 2497 = 6202

16. 206 + 709 + 1342 + 2076 = 4333

17. $190.76 - .99 = $189.77

18. 99,876 - 85,397 = 14,479

19. $876.51 - $92.89 = $783.62

20. 70,935 - 49,489 = 21,446

21. $391.55 - $273.45 = $118.10

22. (2016 + 1634) - 119 = 3650 - 119 = 3531

23. (35)(65)(15) = 34,125

24. (4.06)(.031) = .12586

25. 65 + (14)(13) = 65 + 182 = 247

PREPARING WRITTEN MATERIAL

EXAMINATION SECTION

TEST 1

DIRECTIONS: Each question or incomplete statement is followed by several suggested answers or completions. Select the one that BEST answers the question or completes the statement. *PRINT THE LETTER OF THE CORRECT ANSWER IN THE SPACE AT THE RIGHT.*

1. The one of the following sentences which is LEAST acceptable from the viewpoint of correct usage is:
    A. The police thought the fugitive to be him.
    B. The criminals set a trap for whoever would fall into it.
    C. It is ten years ago since the fugitive fled from the city.
    D. The lecturer argued that criminals are usually cowards.
    E. The police removed four bucketfuls of earth from the scene of the crime.

1._____

2. The one of the following sentences which is LEAST acceptable from the viewpoint of correct usage is:
    A. The patrolman scrutinized the report with great care.
    B. Approaching the victim of the assault, two bruises were noticed by the patrolman.
    C. As soon as I had broken down the door, I stepped into the room.
    D. I observed the accused loitering near the building, which was closed at the time.
    E. The storekeeper complained that his neighbor was guilty of violating a local ordinance.

2._____

3. The one of the following sentences which is LEAST acceptable from the viewpoint of correct usage is:
    A. I realized immediately that he intended to assault the woman, so I disarmed him.
    B. It was apparent that Mr. Smith's explanation contained many inconsistencies.
    C. Despite the slippery condition of the street, he managed to stop the vehicle before injuring the child.
    D. Not a single one of them wish, despite the damage to property, to make a formal complaint.
    E. The body was found lying on the floor.

3._____

4. The one of the following sentences which contains NO error in usage is:
    A. After the robbers left, the proprietor stood tied in his chair for about two hours before help arrived.
    B. In the cellar I found the watchman's hat and coat.
    C. The persons living in adjacent apartments stated that they had heard no unusual noises.

4._____

2 (#1)

D. Neither a knife or any firearms were found in the room.
E. Walking down the street, the shouting of the crowd indicated that something was wrong.

5. The one of the following sentences which contains NO error in usage is:
   A. The policeman lay a firm hand on the suspect's shoulder.
   B. It is true that neither strength nor agility are the most important requirement for a good patrolman.
   C. Good citizens constantly strive to do more than merely comply the restraints imposed by society.
   D. No decision was made as to whom the prize should be awarded.
   E. Twenty years is considered a severe sentence for a felony.

   5._____

6. Which of the following sentences is NOT expressed in standard English usage?
   A. The victim reached a pay-phone booth and manages to call police headquarters.
   B. By the time the call was received, the assailant had left the scene.
   C. The victim has been a respected member of the community for the past eleven years.
   D. Although the lighting was bad and the shadows were deep, the storekeeper caught sight of the attacker.
   E. Additional street lights have since been installed, and the patrols have been strengthened.

   5._____

7. Which of the following sentences is NOT expressed in standard English usage?
   A. The judge upheld the attorney's right to question the witness about the missing glove.
   B. To be absolutely fair to all parties is the jury's chief responsibility.
   C. Having finished the report, a loud noise in the next room startled the sergeant.
   D. The witness obviously enjoyed having played a part in the proceedings.
   E. The sergeant planned to assign the case to whoever arrived first.

   7._____

8. In which of the following sentences is a word misused?
   A. As a matter of principle, the captain insisted that the suspect's partner be brought for questioning.
   B. The principle suspect had been detained at the station house for most of the day.
   C. The principal in the crime had no previous criminal record, but his closest associate had been convicted of felonies on two occasions.
   D. The interest payments had been made promptly, but the firm had been drawing upon the principal for these payments.
   E. The accused insisted that his high school principal would furnish him a character reference.

   8._____

9. Which of the following statements is ambiguous? 9._____
   A. Mr. Sullivan explained why Mr. Johnson had been dismissed from his job.
   B. The storekeeper told the patrolman he had made a mistake.
   C. After waiting three hours, the patients in the doctor's office were sent home.
   D. The janitor's duties were to maintain the building in good shape and to answer tenants' complaints.
   E. The speed limit should, in my opinion, be raised to sixty miles an hour on that stretch of road.

10. In which of the following is the punctuation or capitalization faulty? 10._____
    A. The accident occurred at an intersection in the Kew Gardens section of Queens, near the bus stop.
    B. The sedan, not the convertible, was struck in the side.
    C. Before any of the patrolmen had left the police car received an important message from headquarters.
    D. The dog that had been stolen was returned to his master, John Dempsey, who lived in East Village.
    E. The letter had been sent to 12 Hillside Terrace, Rutland, Vermont 05702.

Questions 11-25.

DIRECTIONS: Questions 11 through 25 are to be answered in accordance with correct English usage; that is, standard English rather than nonstandard or substandard. Nonstandard and substandard English includes words or expressions usually classified as slang, dialect, illiterate, etc., which are not generally accepted as correct in current written communication. Standard English also requires clarity, proper punctuation and capitalization and appropriate use of words. Write the letter of the sentence NOT expressed in standard English usage in the space at the right.

11. A. There were three witnesses to the accident. 11._____
    B. At least three witnesses were found to testify for the plaintiff.
    C. Three of the witnesses who took the stand was uncertain about the defendant's competence to drive.
    D. Only three witnesses came forward to testify for the plaintiff.
    E. The three witnesses to the accident were pedestrians.

12. A. The driver had obviously drunk too many martinis before leaving for home. 12._____
    B. The boy who drowned had swum in these same waters many times before.
    C. The petty thief had stolen a bicycle from a private driveway before he was apprehended.
    D. The detectives had brung in the heroin shipment they intercepted.
    E. The passengers had never ridden in a converted bus before.

13. A. Between you and me, the new platoon plan sounds like a good idea.
    B. Money from an aunt's estate was left to his wife and he.
    C. He and I were assigned to the same patrol for the first time in two months.
    D. Either you or he should check the front door of that store.
    E. The captain himself was not sure of the witness's reliability.

14. A. The alarm had scarcely begun to ring when the explosion occurred.
    B. Before the firemen arrived at the scene, the second story had been destroyed.
    C. Because of the dense smoke and heat, the firemen could hardly approach the now-blazing structure.
    D. According to the patrolman's report, there wasn't nobody in the store when the explosion occurred.
    E. The sergeant's suggestion was not at all unsound, but no one agreed with him.

15. A. The driver and the passenger they were both found to be intoxicated.
    B. The driver and the passenger talked slowly and not too clearly.
    C. Neither the driver nor his passengers were able to give a coherent account of the accident.
    D. In a corner of the room sat the passenger, quietly dozing.
    E. the driver finally told a strange and unbelievable story, which the passenger contradicted.

16. A. Under the circumstances I decided not to continue my examination of the premises.
    B. There are many difficulties now not comparable with those existing in 1960.
    C. Friends of the accused were heard to announce that the witness had better been away on the day of the trial.
    D. The two criminals escaped in the confusion that followed the explosion.
    E. The aged man was struck by the considerateness of the patrolman's offer.

17. A. An assemblage of miscellaneous weapons lay on the table.
    B. Ample opportunities were given to the defendant to obtain counsel.
    C. The speaker often alluded to his past experience with youthful offenders in the armed forces.
    D. The sudden appearance of the truck aroused my suspicions.
    E. Her studying had a good affect on her grades in high school.

18. A. He sat down in the theater and began to watch the movie.
    B. The girl had ridden horses since she was four years old.
    C. Application was made on behalf of the prosecutor to cite the witness for contempt.
    D. The bank robber, with his two accomplices, were caught in the act.
    E. His story is simply not credible.

19.
- A. The angry boy said that he did not like those kind of friends.
- B. The merchant's financial condition was so precarious that he felt he must avail himself of any offer of assistance.
- C. He is apt to promise more than he can perform.
- D. Looking at the messy kitchen, the housewife felt like crying.
- E. A clerk was left in charge of the stolen property.

20.
- A. His wounds were aggravated by prolonged exposure to sub-freezing temperatures.
- B. The prosecutor remarked that the witness was not averse to changing his story each time he was interviewed.
- C. The crime pattern indicated that the burglars were adapt in the handling of explosives.
- D. His rigid adherence to a fixed plan brought him into renewed conflict with his subordinates.
- E. He had anticipated that the sentence would be delivered by noon.

21.
- A. The whole arraignment procedure is badly in need of revision.
- B. After his glasses were broken in the fight, he would of gone to the optometrist if he could.
- C. Neither Tom nor Jack brought his lunch to work.
- D. He stood aside until the quarrel was over.
- E. A statement in the psychiatrist's report disclosed that the probationer vowed to have his revenge.

22.
- A. His fiery and intemperate speech to the striking employees fatally affected any chance of a future reconciliation.
- B. The wording of the statute has been variously construed.
- C. The defendant's attorney, speaking in the courtroom, called the official a demagogue who contempuously disregarded the judge's orders.
- D. The baseball game is likely to be the most exciting one this year.
- E. The mother divided the cookies among her two children.

23.
- A. There was only a bed and a dresser in the dingy room.
- B. John was one of the few students that have protested the new rule.
- C. It cannot be argued that the child's testimony is negligible; it is, on the contrary, of the greatest importance.
- D. The basic criterion for clearance was so general that officials resolved any doubts in favor of dismissal.
- E. Having just returned from a long vacation, the officer found the city unbearably hot.

24.
- A. The librarian ought to give more help to small children.
- B. The small boy was criticized by the teacher because he often wrote careless.
- C. It was generally doubted whether the women would permit the use of her apartment for intelligence operations.
- D. The probationer acts differently every time the officer visits him.
- E. Each of the newly appointed officers has 12 years of service.

25.
A. The North is the most industrialized region in the country.
B. L. Patrick Gray 3d, the bureau's acting director, stated that, while "rehabilitation is fine" for some convicted criminals, "it is a useless gesture for those who resist every such effort."
C. Careless driving, faulty mechanism, narrow or badly kept roads all play their part in causing accidents.
D. The childrens' books were left in the bus.
E. It was a matter of internal security; consequently, he felt no inclination to rescind his previous order.

25._____

KEY (CORRECT ANSWERS)

1.	C		11.	C
2.	B		12.	D
3.	D		13.	B
4.	C		14.	D
5.	E		15.	A
6.	A		16.	C
7.	C		17.	E
8.	B		18.	D
9.	B		19.	A
10.	C		20.	C

21. B
22. E
23. B
24. B
25. D

TEST 2

DIRECTIONS: Each question or incomplete statement is followed by several suggested answers or completions. Select the one that BEST answers the question or completes the statement. *PRINT THE LETTER OF THE CORRECT ANSWER IN THE SPACE AT THE RIGHT.*

Questions 1-6.

DIRECTIONS: Each of Questions 1 through 6 consists of a statement which contains a word (one of those underlined) that is either incorrectly used because it is not in keeping with the meaning the quotation is evidently intended to convey, or is misspelled. There is only one INCORRECT word in each quotation. Of the four underlined words, determine if the first one should be replaced by the word lettered A, the second replaced by the word lettered B, the third replaced by the word lettered C, or the fourth replaced by the word lettered D.

1. Whether one depends on fluorescent or artificial light or both, adequate standards should be maintained by means of systematic tests.
   A. natural   B. safeguards   C. established   D. routine

2. A police officer has to be prepared to assume his knowledge as a social scientist in the community.
   A. forced   B. role   C. philosopher   D. street

3. It is practically impossible to indicate whether a sentence is too long simply by measuring its length.
   A. almost   B. tell   C. very   D. guessing

4. Strong leaders are required to organize a community for delinquency prevention and for dissemination of organized crime and drug addiction.
   A. tactics   B. important   C. control   D. meetings

5. The demonstrators who were taken to the Criminal Courts building in Manhattan (because it was large enough to accommodate them), contended that the arrests were unwarranted.
   A. demonstraters
   B. Manhatten
   C. accomodate
   D. unwarranted

6. They were guaranteed a calm atmosphere, free from harassment, which would be conducive to quiet consideration of the indictments.
   A. guarenteed
   B. atmspher
   C. harassment
   D. inditements

Questions 7-11.

DIRECTIONS: Each of Questions 7 through 11 consists of a statement containing four words in capital letters. One of these words in capital letters is not in keeping with the meaning which the statement is evidently intended to carry. The four words in capital letters in each statement are reprinted after the statement. Print the capital letter preceding the one of the four words which does MOST to spoil the true meaning of the statement in the space at the right.

7. Retirement and pension systems are essential not only to provide employees with with a means of support in the future, but also to prevent longevity and CHARITABLE considerations from UPSETTING the PROMOTIONAL opportunities RETIRED members of the career service. 7.____
   A. charitable   B. upsetting   C. promotional   D. retired

8. Within each major DIVISION in a properly set up public or private organization, provision is made so that each NECESSARY activity is CARED for and lines of authority and responsibility are clear-cut and INFINITE. 8.____
   A. division   B. necessary   C. cared   D. infinite

9. In public service, the scale of salaries paid must be INCIDENTAL to the services rendered, with due CONSIDERATION for the attraction of the desired MANPOWER and for the maintenance of a standard of living COMMENSURATE with the work to be performed. 9.____
   A. incidental   B. consideration
   C. manpower   D. commensurate

10. An understanding of the AIMS of an organization by the staff will AID greatly in increasing the DEMAND of the correspondence work of the office, and will to a large extent DETERMINE the nature of the correspondence. 10.____
    A. aims   B. aid   C. demand   D. determine

11. BECAUSE the Civil Service Commission strongly feels that the MERIT system is a key factor in the MAINTENANCE of democratic government, it has adopted as one of its major DEFENSES the progressive democratization of its own procedures in dealing with candidates for positions in the public service. 11.____
    A. Because   B. merit   C. maintenance   D. defenses

Questions 12-14.

DIRECTIONS: Questions 12 through 14 consist of one sentence each. Each sentence contains an incorrectly used word. First, decide which is the incorrectly used word. Then, from among the options given, decide which word, when substituted for the incorrectly used word, makes the meaning of the sentence clear.
EXAMPLE:
The U.S. national income exhibits a pattern of long term deflection.
   A. reflection   B. subjection   C. rejoicing   D. growth

The word *deflection* in the sentence does not convey the meaning the sentence evidently intended to convey. The word *growth* (Answer D), when substituted for the word *deflection*, makes the meaning of the sentence clear. Accordingly, the answer to the question is D.

12. The study commissioned by the joint committee fell compassionately short of the mark and would have to be redone.
    A. successfully
    B. insignificantly
    C. experimentally
    D. woefully

13. He will not idly exploit any violation of the provisions of the order.
    A. tolerate   B. refuse   C. construe   D. guard

14. The defendant refused to be virile and bitterly protested service.
    A. irked   B. feasible   C. docile   D. credible

Questions 15-25.

DIRECTIONS: Questions 15 through 25 consist of short paragraphs. Each paragraph contains one word which is INCORRECTLY used because it is NOT in keeping with the meaning of the paragraph. Find the word in each paragraph which is INCORRECTLY used and then select as the answer the suggested word which should be substituted for the incorrectly used word.

SAMPLE QUESTION:
In determining who is to do the work in your unit, you will have to decide just who does what from day to day. One of your lowest responsibilities is to assign work so that everybody gets a fair share and that everyone can do his part well.
    A. new   B. old   C. important   D. performance

EXPLANATION:
The word which is NOT in keeping with the meaning of the paragraph is *lowest*. This is the INCORRECTLY used word. The suggested word *important* would be in keeping with the meaning of the paragraph and should be substituted for *lowest*. Therefore, the CORRECT answer is choice C.

15. If really good practice in the elimination of preventable injuries is to be achieved and held in any establishment, top management must refuse full and definite responsibility and must apply a good share of its attention to the task.
    A. accept   B. avoidable   C. duties   D. problem

16. Recording the human face for identification is by no means the only service performed by the camera in the field of investigation. When the trial of any issue takes place, a word picture is sought to be distorted to the court of incidents, occurrences, or events which are in dispute.
    A. appeals   B. description   C. portrayed   D. deranged

4 (#2)

17. In the collection of physical evidence, it cannot be emphasized too strongly that a haphazard systematic search at the scene of the crime is vital. Nothing must be overlooked. Often the only leads in a case will come from the results of this search.
    A. important
    B. investigation
    C. proof
    D. thorough

    17._____

18. If an investigator has reason to suspect that the witness is mentally stable, or a habitual drunkard, he should leave no stone unturned in his investigation to determine if the witness was under the influence of liquor or drugs, or was mentally unbalanced either at the time of the occurrence to which he testified or at the time of the trial.
    A. accused
    B. clue
    C. deranged
    D. question

    18._____

19. The use of records is a valuable step in crime investigation and is the main reason every department should maintain accurate reports. Crimes are not committed through the use of departmental records alone but from the use of all records, of almost every type, wherever they may be found and whenever they give any incidental information regarding the criminal.
    A. accidental
    B. necessary
    C. reported
    D. solved

    19._____

20. In the years since passage of the Harrison Narcotic Act of 1914, making the possession of opium amphetamines illegal in most circumstances, drug use has become a subject of considerable scientific interest and investigation. There is at present a voluminous literature on drug use of various kinds.
    A. ingestion
    B. derivatives
    C. addiction
    D. opiates

    20._____

21. Of course, the fact that criminal laws are extremely patterned in definition does not mean that the majority of persons who violate them are dealt with as criminals. Quite the contrary, for a great many forbidden acts are voluntarily engaged in within situations of privacy and go unobserved and unreported.
    A. symbolic
    B. casual
    C. scientific
    D. broad-gauged

    21._____

22. The most punitive way to study punishment is to focus attention on the pattern of punitive action: to study how a penalty is applied, too study what is done to or taken from an offender.
    A. characteristic
    B. degrading
    C. objective
    D. distinguished

    22._____

23. The most common forms of punishment in times past have been death, physical torture, mutilation, branding, public humiliation, fines, forfeits of property, banishment, transportation, and imprisonment. Although this list is by no means differentiated, practically every form of punishment has had several variations and applications.
    A. specific
    B. simple
    C. exhaustive
    D. characteristic

    23._____

24. There is another important line of inference between ordinary and professional criminals, and that is the source from which they are recruited. The professional criminal seems to be drawn from legitimate employment and, in many instances, from parallel vocations or pursuits.
    A. demarcation   B. justification   C. superiority   D. reference

    24._____

25. He took the position that the success of the program was insidious on getting additional revenue.
    A. reputed   B. contingent   C. failure   D. indeterminate

    25._____

KEY (CORRECT ANSWERS)

1.	A	11.	D
2.	B	12.	D
3.	B	13.	A
4.	C	14.	C
5.	D	15.	A
6.	C	16.	C
7.	D	17.	D
8.	D	18.	C
9.	A	19.	D
10.	C	20.	B

21.	D
22.	C
23.	C
24.	A
25.	B

TEST 3

DIRECTIONS: Each question or incomplete statement is followed by several suggested answers or completions. Select the one that BEST answers the question or completes the statement. *PRINT THE LETTER OF THE CORRECT ANSWER IN THE SPACE AT THE RIGHT.*

Questions 1-5.

DIRECTIONS: Questions 1 through 5 are to be answered on the basis of the following.

You are a supervising officer in an investigative unit. Earlier in the day, you directed Detectives Tom Dixon and Sal Mayo to investigate a reported assault and robbery in a liquor store within your area of jurisdiction.

Detective Dixon has submitted to you a preliminary investigative report containing the following information:

- At 1630 hours on 2/20, arrived at Joe's Liquor Store at 350 SW Avenue with Detective Mayo to investigate A & R.
- At store interviewed Rob Ladd, store manager, who stated that he and Joe Brown (store owner) had been stuck up about ten minutes prior to our arrival.
- Ladd described the robbers as male whites in their late teens or early twenties. Further stated that one of the robbers displayed what appeared to be an automatic pistol as he entered the store, and said, *Give us the money or we'll kill you.* Ladd stated that Brown then reached under the counter where he kept a loaded .38 caliber pistol. Several shots followed, and Ladd threw himself to the floor.
- The robbers fled, and Ladd didn't know if any money had been taken.
- At this point, Ladd realized that Brown was unconscious on the floor and bleeding from a head wound.
- Ambulance called by Ladd, and Brown was removed by same to General Hospital.
- Personally interviewed John White, 382 Dartmouth Place, who stated he was inside store at the time of occurrence. White states that he hid behind a wine display upon hearing someone say, *Give us the money.* He then heard shots and saw two young men run from the store to a yellow car parked at the curb. White was unable to further describe auto. States the taller of the two men drove the car away while the other sat on passenger side in front.
- Recovered three spent .38 caliber bullets from premises and delivered them to Crime Lab.
- To General Hospital at 1800 hours but unable to interview Brown, who was under sedation and suffering from shock and a laceration of the head.
- Alarm #12487 transmitted for car and occupants.
- Case Active.

Based solely on the contents of the preliminary investigation submitted by Detective Dixon, select one sentence from the following groups of sentences which is MOST accurate and is grammatically correct.

1. A. Both robbers were armed.
    B. Each of the robbers were described as a male white.
    C. Neither robber was armed.
    D. Mr. Ladd stated that one of the robbers was armed.

2. A. Mr. Brown fired three shots from his revolver.
    B. Mr. Brown was shot in the head by one of the robbers.
    C. Mr. Brown suffered a gunshot wound of the head during the course of the robbery.
    D. Mr. Brown was taken to General Hospital by ambulance.

3. A. Shots were fired after one of the robbers said, *Give us the money or we'll kill you.*
    B. After one of the robbers demanded the money from Mr. Brown, he fired a shot.
    C. The preliminary investigation indicated that although Mr. Brown did not have a license for the gun, he was justified in using deadly physical force.
    D. Mr. Brown was interviewed at General Hospital.

4. A. Each of the witnesses were customers in the store at the time of occurrence.
    B. Neither of the witnesses interviewed was the owner of the liquor store.
    C. Neither of the witnesses interviewed were the owner of the store.
    D. Neither of the witnesses was employed by Mr. Brown.

5. A. Mr. Brown arrived at General Hospital at about 5:00 P.M.
    B. Neither of the robbers was injured during the robbery.
    C. The robbery occurred at 3:30 P.M. on February 10.
    D. One of the witnesses called the ambulance.

Questions 6-10.

DIRECTIONS: Each of Questions 6 through 10 consists of information given in outline form and four sentences labeled A, B, C, and D. For each question, choose the one sentence which CORRECTLY expresses the information given in outline form and which also displays PROPER English usage.

6. Client's Name: Joanna Jones
    Number of Children: 3
    Client's Income: None
    Client's Marital Status: Single

    A. Joanna Jones is an unmarried client with three children who have no income.
    B. Joanna Jones, who is single and has no income, a client she has three children.
    C. Joanna Jones, whose three children are clients, is single and has no income.
    D. Joanna Jones, who has three children, is an unmarried client with no income.

3 (#3)

7. Client's Name: Bertha Smith
   Number of Children: 2
   Client's Rent: $1050 per month
   Number of Rooms: 4

   7._____

   A. Bertha Smith, a client, pays $1050 per month for her four rooms with two children.
   B. Client Bertha Smith has two children and pays $1050 per month for four rooms.
   C. Client Bertha Smith is paying $1050 per month for two children with four rooms.
   D. For four rooms and two children client Bertha Smith pays $1050 per month.

8. Name of Employee: Cynthia Dawes
   Number of Cases Assigned: 9
   Date Cases were Assigned: 12/16
   Number of Assigned Cases Completed: 8

   8._____

   A. On December 16, employee Cynthia Dawes was assigned nine cases; she has completed eight of these cases.
   B. Cynthia Dawes, employee on December 16, assigned nine cases, completed eight.
   C. Being employed on December 16, Cynthia Dawes completed eight of nine assigned cases.
   D. Employee Cynthia Dawes, she was assigned nine cases and completed eight, on December 16.

9. Place of Audit: Broadway Center
   Names of Auditors: Paul Cahn, Raymond Perez
   Date of Audit: 11/20
   Number of Cases Audited: 41

   9._____

   A. On November 20, at the Broadway Center 41 cases was audited by auditors Paul Cahn and Raymond Perez.
   B. Auditors Raymond Perez and Paul Cahn has audited 41 cases at the Broadway Center on November 20.
   C. At the Broadway Center, on November 20, auditors Paul Cahn and Raymond Perez audited 41 cases.
   D. Auditors Paul Cahn and Raymond Perez at the Broadway Center, on November 20, is auditing 41 cases.

10. Name of Client: Barbra Levine
    Client's Monthly Income: $2100
    Client's Monthly Expenses: $4520

    10._____

    A. Barbra Levine is a client, her monthly income is $2100 and her monthly expenses is $4520.
    B. Barbra Levine's monthly income is $2100 and she is a client, with whose monthly expenses are $4520.

C. Barbra Levine is a client whose monthly income is $2100 and whose monthly expenses are $4520.
D. Barbra Levine, a client, is with a monthly income which is $2100 and monthly expenses which are $4520.

Questions 11-13.

DIRECTIONS: Questions 11 through 13 involve several statements of fact presented in a very simple way. These statements of fact are followed by 4 choices which attempt to incorporate all of the facts into one logical statement which is properly constructed and grammatically correct.

11. I. Mr. Brown was sweeping the sidewalk in front of his house.
    II. He was sweeping it because it was dirty.
    III. He swept the refuse into the street.
    IV. Police Officer gave him a ticket.

    Which one of the following BEST presents the information given above?
    A. Because his sidewalk was dirty, Mr. Brown received a ticket from Officer Green when he swept the refuse into the street.
    B. Police Officer Green gave Mr. Brown a ticket because his sidewalk was dirty and he swept the refuse into the street.
    C. Police Officer Green gave Mr. Brown a ticket for sweeping refuse into the street because his sidewalk was dirty.
    D. Mr. Brown, who was sweeping refuse from his dirty sidewalk into the street, was given a ticket by Police Officer Green.

11._____

12. I. Sergeant Smith radioed for help.
    II. The sergeant did so because the crowd was getting larger.
    III. It was 10:00 A.M. when he made his call.
    IV. Sergeant Smith was not in uniform at the time of occurrence.

    Which one of the following BEST presents the information given above?
    A. Sergeant Smith, although not on duty at the time, radioed for help at 10 o'clock because the crowd was getting uglier.
    B. Although not in uniform, Sergeant Smith called for help at 10:00 A.M. because the crowd was getting uglier.
    C. Sergeant Smith radioed for help at 10:00 A.M. because the crowd was getting larger.
    D. Although he was not in uniform, Sergeant Smith radioed for help at 10:00 A.M. because the crowd was getting larger.

12._____

13. I. The payroll office is open on Fridays.
    II. Paychecks are distributed from 9:00 A.M. to 12 Noon.
    III. The office is open on Fridays because that's the only day the payroll staff is available.
    IV. It is open for the specified hours in order to permit employees to cash checks at the bank during lunch hour.

13._____

The choice below which MOST clearly and accurately presents the above idea is:
- A. Because the payroll office is open on Fridays from 9:00 A.M. to 12 Noon, employees can cash their checks when the payroll staff is available.
- B. Because the payroll staff is only available on Fridays until noon, employees can cash their checks during their lunch hour.
- C. Because the payroll staff is available only on Fridays, the office is open from 9:00 A.M. to 12 Noon to allow employees to cash their checks.
- D. Because of payroll staff availability, the payroll office is open on Fridays. It is open from 9:00 A.M. to 12 Noon so that distributed paychecks can be cashed at the bank while employees are on their lunch hour.

Questions 14-16.

DIRECTIONS: In each of Questions 14 through 6, the four sentences are from a paragraph in a report. They are not in the right order. Which of the following arrangements is the BEST one?

14. I. An executive may answer a letter by writing his reply on the face of the letter itself instead of having a return letter typed.
    II. This procedure is efficient because it saves the executive's time, the typist's time, and saves office file space.
    III. Copying machines are used in small offices as well as large offices to save time and money in making brief replies to business letters.
    IV. A copy is made on a copy machine to go into the company files, while the original is mailed back to the sender.

    The CORRECT answer is:
    A. I, II, IV, III   B. I, IV, II, III   C. III, I, IV, II   D. III, IV, II, I

14.____

15. I. Most organizations favor one of the types but always include the others to a lesser degree.
    II. However, we can detect a definite trend toward greater use of symbolic control.
    III. We suggest that our local police agencies are today primarily utilizing material control.
    IV. Control can be classified into three types: physical, material, and symbolic.

    The CORRECT answer is:
    A. IV, II, III, I   B. II, I, IV, III   C. III, IV, II, I   D. IV, I, III, II

15.____

16. I. They can and do take advantage of ancient political and geographical boundaries, which often give them sanctuary from effective policy activity.
    II. This country is essentially a country of small police forces, each operating independently within the limits of its jurisdiction.
    III. The boundaries that define and limit police operations do not hinder the movement of criminals, of course.
    IV. The machinery of law enforcement in America is fragmented, complicated, and frequently overlapping.

16.____

The CORRECT answer is:
A. III, I, IV   B. II, IV, I, III   C. IV, II, III, I   D. IV, III, II, I

17. Examine the following sentence, and then choose from below the words which should be inserted in the blank spaces to produce the best sentence.
    The unit has exceeded _____ goals and the employees are satisfied with _____ accomplishments.
    A. their, it's   B. it's; it's   C. its, there   D. its, their

18. Examine the following sentence, and then choose from below the words which should be inserted in the blank spaces to produce the best sentence.
    Research indicates that employees who _____ no opportunity for close social relationships often find their work unsatisfying, and this _____ of satisfaction often reflects itself in low production.
    A. have; lack   B. have; excess   C. has; lack   D. has; excess

19. Words in a sentence must be arranged properly to make sure that the intended meaning of the sentence is clear.
    The sentence below that does NOT make sense because a clause has been separated from the word on which its meaning depends is:
    A. To be a good writer, clarity is necessary.
    B. To be a good writer, you must write clearly.
    C. You must write clearly to be a good writer.
    D. Clarity is necessary to good writing.

Questions 20-21.

DIRECTIONS: Each of Questions 20 and 21 consists of a statement which contains a word (one of those underlined) that is either incorrectly used because it is not in keeping with the meaning the quotation is evidently intended to convey, or is misspelled. There is only one INCORRECT word in each quotation. Of the four underlined words, determine if the first one should be replaced by the word lettered A, the second one replaced by the word lettered B, the third one replaced by the word lettered C, or the fourth one replaced by the word lettered D.

20. The alleged killer was occasionally permitted to excercise in the corridor.
    A. alledged   B. ocasionally   C. permited   D. exercise

21. Defense counsel stated, in affect, that their conduct was permissible under the First Amendment.
    A. council   B. effect   C. there   D. permissable

Question 22.

DIRECTIONS: Question 22 consists of one sentence. This sentence contains an incorrectly used word. First, decide which is the incorrectly used word. Then, from among the options given, decide which word, when substituted for the incorrectly used word, makes the meaning of the sentence clear.

22. As today's violence has no single cause, so its causes have no single scheme. 22._____
    A. deference   B. cure   C. flaw   D. relevance

23. In the sentence, *A man in a light-grey suit waited thirty-five minutes in the ante-room for the all-important document*, the word IMPROPERLY hyphenated is 23._____
    A. light-grey   B. thirty-five
    C. ante-room   D. all-important

24. In the sentence, *The candidate wants to file his application for preference before it is too late*, the word *before* is used as a(n) 24._____
    A. preposition   B. subordinating conjunction
    C. pronoun   D. adverb

25. In the sentence, *The perpetrators ran from the scene*, the word *from* is a 25._____
    A. preposition   B. pronoun   C. verb   D. conjunction

KEY (CORRECT ANSWERS)

1.	D		11.	D
2.	D		12.	D
3.	A		13.	D
4.	B		14.	C
5.	D		15.	D
6.	D		16.	C
7.	B		17.	D
8.	A		18.	A
9.	C		19.	A
10.	C		20.	D

21. B
22. B
23. C
24. B
25. A

PREPARING WRITTEN MATERIAL

PARAGRAPH REARRANGEMENT
COMMENTARY

The sentences that follow are in scrambled order. You are to rearrange them in proper order and indicate the letter choice containing the correct answer at the space at the right.

Each group of sentences in this section is actually a paragraph presented in scrambled order. Each sentence in the group has a place in that paragraph; no sentence is to be left out. You are to read each group of sentences and decide upon the best order in which to put the sentences so as to form a well-organized paragraph.

The questions in this section measure the ability to solve a problem when all the facts relevant to its solution are not given.

More specifically, certain positions of responsibility and authority require the employee to discover connection between events sometimes, apparently, unrelated. In order to do this, the employee will find it necessary to correctly infer that unspecified events have probably occurred or are likely to occur. This ability becomes especially important when action must be taken on incomplete information.

Accordingly, these questions require competitors to choose among several suggested alternatives, each of which presents a different sequential arrangement of the events. Competitors must choose the MOST logical of the suggested sequences.

In order to do so, they may be required to draw on general knowledge to infer missing concepts or events that are essential to sequencing the given events. Competitors should be careful to infer only what is essential to the sequence. The plausibility of the wrong alternatives will always require the inclusion of unlikely events or of additional chains of events which are NOT essential to sequencing the given events.

It's very important to remember that you are looking for the best of the four possible choices, and that the best choice of all may not even be one of the answers you're given to choose from.

There is no one right way to solve these problems. Many people have found it helpful to first write out the order of the sentences, as they would have arranged them, on their scrap paper before looking at the possible answers. If their optimum answer is there, this can save them some time. If it isn't, this method can still give insight into solving the problem. Others find it most helpful to just go through each of the possible choices, contrasting each as they go along. You should use whatever method feels comfortable and works for you.

While most of these types of questions are not that difficult, we've added a higher percentage of the difficult type, just to give you more practice. Usually there are only one or two questions on this section that contain such subtle distinctions that you're unable to answer confidently. And you then may find yourself stuck deciding between two possible choices, neither of which you're sure about.

PREPARING WRITTEN MATERIAL
PARAGRAPH REARRANGEMENT

EXAMINATION SECTION

TEST 1

DIRECTIONS: The sentences that follow are in scrambled order. You are to rearrange them in proper order and indicate the letter choice containing the CORRECT answer. *PRINT THE LETTER OF THE CORRECT ANSWER IN THE SPACE AT THE RIGHT.*

1. Police Officer Jenner responds to the scene of a burglary at 2106 La Vista Boulevard. He is approached by an elderly man named Richard Jenkins, whose account of the incident includes the following five sentences:
   I. I saw that the lock on my apartment door had been smashed and the door was open.
   II. My apartment was a shambles; my belongings were everywhere and my television set was missing.
   III. As I walked down the hallway toward the bedroom, I heard someone opening a window.
   IV. I left work at 5:30 P.M. and took the bus home.
   V. At that time, I called the police.
   The MOST logical order for the above sentence to appear in the report is
   A. I, V, IV, II, III   B. IV, I, II, III, V   C. I, V, II, III, IV   D. IV, III, II, V, I

1.____

2. Police Officer LaJolla is writing an Incident Report in which back-up assistance was required. The report will contain the following five sentences:
   I. The radio dispatcher asked what my location was and he then dispatched patrol cars for back-up assistance.
   II. At approximately 9:30 P.M., while I was walking my assigned footpost, a gunman fired three shots at me.
   III. I quickly turned around and saw a white male, approximately 5'10", with black hair, wearing blue jeans, a yellow T-shirt, and white sneaker, running across the avenue carrying a handgun.
   IV. When the back-up officers arrived, we searched the area but could not find the suspect.
   V. I advised the radio dispatcher that a gunman had just fired a gun at me, and then I gave the dispatcher a description of the man
   The MOST logical order for the above sentences to appear in the report is:
   A. III, V, II, IV, I   B. II, III, V, I, IV   C. III, II, IV, I, V   D. II, V, I, III, IV

2.____

3. Police Officer Durant is completing a report of a robbery and assault. The report will contain the following five sentences:
   I. I went to Mount Snow Hospital to interview a man who was attacked and robbed of his wallet earlier that night.
   II. An ambulance arrived at 82nd Street and 3rd Avenue and took an intoxicated, wounded man to Mount Snow Hospital
   III. Two youths attacked the man and stole his wallet.

3.____

IV. A well-dressed man left Hanratty's Bar very drunk, with his wallet hanging out of his back pocket.
V. A passerby dialed 911 and requested police and ambulance assistance.
The MOST logical order for the above sentences to appear in the report is
A. I, II, IV, III, V   B. IV, III, V, II, I   C. IV, V, II, III, I   D. V, IV, III, II, I

4. Police Officer Boswell is preparing a report of an armed robbery and assault which will contain the following five sentences:
I. Both men approached the bartender and one of them drew a gun.
II. The bartender immediately went to grab the phone at the bar.
III. One of the men leaped over the counter and smashed a bottle over the bartender's head.
IV. Two men in a blue Buick drove up to the bar and went inside.
V. I found the cash register empty and the bartender unconscious on the floor, with the phone still dangling off the hook.
The MOST logical order for the above sentences to appear in the report is
A. IV, I, II, II, V   B. V, IV, III, I, II   C. IV, III, II, V, I   D. II, I, III, IV, V

5. Police Officer Mitzler is preparing a report of a bank robbery, which will contain the following five sentences:
I. The teller complied with the instructions on the note, but also hit the silent alarm.
II. The perpetrator then fled south on Broadway.
III. A suspicious male entered the bank at approximately 10:45 A.M.
IV. At this time, an undetermined amount of money has been taken.
V. He approached the teller on the far right side and handed her a note.
The MOST logical order for the above sentences to appear in the report is:
A. III, V, I, II, IV   B. I, III, V, II, IV   C. III, V, IV, I, II   D. III, V, II, IV, I

6. A Police Officer is preparing an Accident Report for an accident which occurred at the intersection of East 119th Street and Lexington Avenue. The report will include the following five sentences:
I. On September 18, while driving ten children to school, a school bus driver passed out.
II. Upon arriving at the scene, I notified the dispatcher to send an ambulance.
III. I notified the parents of each child once I got to the station house.
IV. He said the school bus, while traveling west on East 119th Street, struck a parked Ford which was on the southwest corner of East 119th Street.
V. A witness by the name of John Ramos came up to me to describe what happened.
The MOST logical order for the above sentences to appear in the Accident Report is:
A. I, II, V, III, IV   B. I, II, V, IV, III   C. II, V, I, III, IV   D. II, V, I, IV, III

7. A Police Officer is preparing a report concerning a dispute. The report will contain the following five sentences:
I. The passenger got out of the back of the taxi and leaned through the front window to complain to the driver about the fare.

II. The driver of the taxi caught up with the passenger and knocked him to the ground; the passenger then kicked the driver and a scuffle ensued.
III. The taxi drew up in front of the high-rise building and stopped.
IV. The driver got out of the taxi and followed the passenger into the lobby of the apartment building.
V. The doorman tried but was unable to break up the fight, at which point he called the precinct.

The MOST logical order for the above sentences to appear in the report is
   A. III, I, IV, II, V   B. III, IV, I, II, V   C. III, IV, II, V, I   D. V, I, III, IV, II

8. Police Officer Morrow is writing an Incident Report. The report will include the following four sentences:
I. The man reached into his pocket and pulled out a gun.
II. While on foot patrol, I identified a suspect, who was wanted for six robberies in the area, from a wanted picture I was carrying.
III. I drew my weapon and fired six rounds at the suspect, killing him instantly.
IV. I called for back-up assistance and told the man to put his hands up.

The MOST logical order for the above sentences to appear in the report is
   A. II, III, IV, I   B. IV, I, III, II   C. IV, I, II, III   D. II, IV, I, III

9. Sergeant Allen responds to a call at 16 Grove Street regarding a missing child. At the scene, the Sergeant is met by Police Officer Samuels, who gives a brief account of the incident consisting of the following five sentences:
I. I transmitted the description and waited for you to arrive before I began searching the area.
II. Mrs. Banks, the mother, reports that she last saw her daughter Julie about 7:30 A.M. when she took her to school.
III. About 6 P.M., my partner and I arrived at this location to investigate a report of a missing 8-year-old girl.
IV. When Mrs. Banks left her, Julie was wearing a red and white striped T-shirt, blue jeans, and white sneakers.
V. Mrs. Banks dropped her off in front of the playground of P.S. 11.

The MOST logical order for the above sentences to appear in the report is
   A. III, V, IV, II, I   B. III, II, V, IV, I   C. III, IV, I, II, V   D. III, II, IV, I, V

10. Police Officer Franco is completing a report of an assault. The report will contain the following five sentences:
I. In the park I observed an elderly man lying on the ground, bleeding from a back wound.
II. I applied first aid to control the bleeding and radioed for an ambulance to respond.
III. The elderly man stated that he was sitting on the park bench when he was attacked from behind by two males.
IV. I received a report of a man's screams coming from inside the park, and I went to investigate.
V. The old man could not give a description of his attackers.

The MOST logical order for the above sentences to appear in the report is
   A. IV, I, II, III, V   B. V, III, I, IV, II   C. IV, III, V, II, I   D. II, I, V, IV, III

11. Police Officer Williams is completing a Crime Report. The report contains the following five sentences:
    I. As Police Officer Hanson and I approached the store, we noticed that the front door was broken.
    II. After determining that the burglars had fled, we notified the precinct of the burglary.
    III. I walked through the front door as Police Officer Hanson walked around to the back.
    IV. At approximately midnight, an alarm was heard at the Apex Jewelry Store.
    V. We searched the store and found no one.
    The MOST logical order for the above sentences to appear in the report is
    A. I, IV, II, III, V   B. I, IV, III, V, II   C. IV, I, III, II, V   D. IV, I, III, V, II

12. Police Officer Clay is giving a report to the news media regarding someone who has jumped from the Empire State Building. His report will include the following five sentences:
    I. I responded to the 86th floor, where I found the person at the edge of the roof.
    II. A security guard at the building had reported that a man was on the roof at the 86th floor.
    III. At 5:30 P.M., the person jumped from the building.
    IV. I received a call from the radio dispatcher at 4:50 P.M. to respond to the Empire State Building.
    V. I tried to talk to the person and convince him not to jump.
    The MOST logical order for the above sentences to appear in the report is
    A. I, II, IV, III, V   B. III, IV, I, II, V   C. II, IV, I, III, V   D. IV, II, I, V, III

13. The following five sentences are part of a report of a burglary written by Police Officer Reed:
    I. When I arrived at 2400 1st Avenue, I noticed that the door was slightly open.
    II. I yelled out, *Police, don't move!*
    III. As I entered the apartment, I saw a man with a TV set passing through a window to another man standing on a fire escape.
    IV. While on foot patrol, I was informed by the radio dispatcher that a burglary was in progress at 2400 1st Avenue.
    V. However, the burglars quickly ran down the fire escape.
    The MOST logical order for the above sentences to appear in the report is
    A. I, III, IV, V, II   B. IV, I, III, V, II   C. IV, I, III, II, V   D. I, IV, III, II, V

14. Police Officer Jenkins is preparing a report for Lost or Stolen Property. The report will include the following five sentences:
    I. On the stairs, Mr. Harris slipped on a wet leaf and fell on the landing.
    II. It wasn't until he got to the token booth that Mr. Harris realized his wallet was no longer in his back pants pocket.
    III. A boy wearing a football jersey helped him up and brushed off the back of Mr. Harris' pants.
    IV. Mr. Harris states he was walking up the stairs to the elevated subway at Queensborough Plaza.
    V. Before Mr. Harris could thank him, the boy was running down the stairs to the street.

The MOST logical order for the above sentences to appear in the report is
A. IV, III, V, I, II   B. IV, I, III, V, II   C. I, IV, II, III, V   D. I, II, IV, III, V

15. Police Officer Hubbard is completing a report of a missing person. The report will contain the following five sentences:
    I. I visited the store at 7:55 P.M. and asked the employees if they had seen a girl fitting the description I had been given.
    II. She gave me a description and said she had gone into the local grocery store at about 6:15 P.M.
    III. I asked the woman for a description of her daughter.
    IV. The distraught woman called the precinct to report that her daughter, aged 12, had not returned from an errand.
    V. The storekeeper said a girl matching the description had been in the store earlier, but he could not give an exact time.
    The MOST logical order for the above sentences to appear in the report is
    A. I, III, II, V, IV   B. IV, III, II, I, V   C. V, I, II, III, IV   D. III, I, II, IV, V

16. A police officer is completing an entry in his Daily Activity Log regarding traffic summonses which he issued. The following five sentences will be included in the entry:
    I. I was on routine patrol parked 16 yards west of 170th Street and Clay Avenue.
    II. The summonses were issued for unlicensed operator and disobeying a steady red light.
    III. At 8 A.M. hours, I observed an auto traveling westbound on 170th Street not stop for a steady red light at the intersection of Clay Avenue and 170th Street.
    IV. I stopped the driver of the auto and determined that he did not have a valid driver's license.
    V. After a brief conversation, I informed the motorist that he was receiving two summonses.
    The MOST logical order for the above sentences to appear in the report is
    A. I, III, IV, V, II   B. III, IV, II, V, I   C. V, II, I, III, IV   D. IV, V, II, I, III

17. The following sentences appeared on an Incident Report:
    I. Three teenagers who had been ejected from the theater were yelling at patrons who were now entering.
    II. Police Officer Dixon told the teenagers to leave the area.
    III. The teenager said that they were told by the manager to leave the theater because they were talking during the movie.
    IV. The theater manager called the precinct at 10:20 P.M. to report a disturbance outside the theater.
    V. A patrol car responded to the theater at 10:42 P.M. and two police officers went over to the teenagers.
    The MOST logical order for the above sentences to appear in the Incident Report is
    A. I, V, IV, III, II   B. IV, I, V, III, II   C. IV, I, III, V, II   D. IV, III, I, V, II

18. Activity Log entries are completed by police officers. Police Officer Samuels has written an entry concerning vandalism and part of it contains the following five sentences:
    I. The man, in his early twenties, ran down the block and around the corner.
    II. A man passing the store threw a brick through a window of the store.
    III. I arrived on the scene and began to question the witnesses about the incident.
    IV. Malcolm Holmes, the owner of the Fast Service Shoe Repair Store, was working in the back of the store at approximately 3 P.M.
    V. After the man fled, Mr. Holmes called the police.
    The MOST logical order for the above sentences to appear in the Activity Log is
    A. IV, II, I, V, III   B. II, IV, I, III, V   C. II, I, IV, III, V   D. IV, II, V, III, I

19. Police Officer Buckley is preparing a report concerning a dispute in a restaurant. The report will contain the following five sentences:
    I. The manager, Charles Chin, and a customer, Edward Green, were standing near the register arguing over the bill.
    II. The manager refused to press any charges providing Green pay the check and leave.
    III. While on foot patrol, I was informed by a passerby of a disturbance in the Dragon Flame Restaurant.
    IV. Green paid the $15.00 check and left the restaurant.
    V. According to witnesses, the customer punched the owner in the face when Chin asked him for the amount due.
    The MOST logical order for the above sentences to appear in the report is
    A. III, I, V, II, IV   B. I, II, III, IV, V   C. V, I, III, II, IV   D. III, V, II, IV, I

20. Police Officer Wilkins is preparing a report for leaving the scene of an accident. The report will include the following five sentences:
    I. The Dodge struck the right rear fender of Mrs. Smith's 2010 Ford and continued on its way.
    II. Mrs. Smith stated she was making a left turn from 40th Street onto Third Avenue.
    III. As the car passed, Mrs. Smith noticed the dangling rear license plate #412AEJ.
    IV. Mrs. Smith complained to police of back pains and was removed by ambulance to Bellevue Hospital.
    V. An old green Dodge traveling up Third Avenue went through the red light at 40th Street and Third Avenue.
    The MOST logical order for the above sentences to appear in the report is
    A. V, III, I, II, IV   B. I, III, II, V, IV   C. IV, V, I, II, III   D. II, V, I, III, IV

21. Detective Simon is completing a Crime Report. The report contains the following five sentences:
    I. Police Officer Chin, while on foot patrol, heard the yelling and ran in the direction of the man.
    II. The man, carrying a large hunting knife, left the High Sierra Sporting Goods Store at approximately 10:30 A.M.

III. When the man heard Police Officer Chin, he stopped, dropped the knife, and began to cry.
IV. As Police Officer Chin approached the man, he drew his gun and yelled, *Police, freeze.*
V. After the man left the store, he began yelling, over and over, *I am going to kill myself!*

The MOST logical order for the above sentences to appear in the report is
   A. V, II, I, IV, III   B. II, V, I, IV, III   C. II, V, IV, I, III   D. II, I, V, IV, III

22. Police Officer Miller is preparing a Complaint Report which will include the following five sentences:
    I. From across the lot, he yelled to the boys to get away from his car.
    II. When he came out of the store, he noticed two teenage boys trying to break into his car.
    III. The boys fled as Mr. Johnson ran to his car.
    IV. Mr. Johnson stated that he parked his car in the municipal lot behind Tams Department Store.
    V. Mr. Johnson saw that the door lock had been broken, but nothing was missing from inside the auto.

    The MOST logical order for the above sentences to appear in the report is
       A. IV, I, II, V, III   B. II, III, I, V, IV   C. IV, II, I, III, V   D. I, II, III, V, IV

23. Police Officer O'Hara completes a Universal Summons for a motorist who has just passed a red traffic light. The Universal Summons includes the following five sentences:
    I. As the car passed the light, I followed in the patrol car.
    II. After the driver stopped the car, he stated that the light was yellow, not red.
    III. A blue Cadillac sedan passed the red light on the corner of 79th Street and 3rd Avenue at 11:25 P.M.
    IV. As a result, the driver was informed that he did pass a red light and that his brake lights were not working.
    V. The driver in the Cadillac stopped his car as soon as he saw the patrol car, and I noticed that the brake lights were not working.

    The MOST logical order for the above sentences to appear in the Universal Summons is
       A. I, III, V, II, IV   B. III, I, V, II, IV   C. III, I, V, IV, II   D. I, III, IV, II, V

24. Detective Egan is preparing a follow-up report regarding a homicide on 170th Street and College Avenue. An unknown male was found at the scene. The report will contain the following five sentences:
    I. Police Officer Gregory wrote down the names, addresses, and phone numbers of the witnesses.
    II. A 911 operator received a call of a man shot and dispatched Police Officers Worth and Gregory to the scene.
    III. They discovered an unidentified male dead on the street.
    IV. Police Officer Worth notified the Precinct Detective Unit immediately.
    V. At approximately 9:00 A.M., an unidentified male shot another male in the chest during an argument.

The MOST logical order for the above sentences to appear in the report is
A. V, II, III, IV, I   B. II, III, V, IV, I   C. IV, I, V, II, III   D. V, III, II, IV, I

25. Police Officer Tracey is preparing a Robbery Report which will include the following five sentences:
   I. I ran around the corner and observe a man pointing a gun at a taxidriver.
   II. I informed the man I was a police officer and that he should not move.
   III. I was on the corner of 125th Street and Park Avenue when I heard a scream coming from around the corner.
   IV. The man turned around and fired one shot at me.
   V. I fired once, shooting him in the arm and causing him to fall to the ground.
   The MOST logical order for the above sentences to appear in the report is
   A. I, III, IV, II, V   B. IV, V, II, I, III   C. III, I, II, IV, V   D. III, I, V, II, IV

25.____

KEY (CORRECT ANSWERS)

1.	B	11.	D
2.	B	12.	D
3.	B	13.	C
4.	A	14.	B
5.	A	15.	B
6.	B	16.	A
7.	A	17.	B
8.	D	18.	A
9.	B	19.	A
10.	A	20.	D

21.	B
22.	C
23.	B
24.	A
25.	C

TEST 2

DIRECTIONS: The sentences that follow are in scrambled order. You are to rearrange them in proper order and indicate the letter choice containing the CORRECT answer. *PRINT THE LETTER OF THE CORRECT ANSWER IN THE SPACE AT THE RIGHT*

1. Police Officer Weiker is completing a Complaint Report which will contain the following five sentences:
   I. Mr. Texlor was informed that the owner of the van would receive a parking ticket and that the van would be towed away.
   II. The police tow truck arrived approximately one half hour after Mr. Texlor complained.
   III. While on foot patrol on West End Avenue, I saw the owner of Rand's Restaurant arrive to open his business.
   IV. Mr. Texlor, the owner, called to me and complained that he could not receive deliveries because a van was blocking his driveway.
   V. The van's owner later reported to the precinct that his van had been stolen, and he was then informed that it had been towed.
   The MOST logical order for the above sentences to appear in the report is
   A. III, V, I, II, IV   B. III, IV, I, II, V   C. IV, III, I, II, V   D. IV, III, II, I, V

1.____

2. Police Officer Ames is completing an entry in his Activity Log. The entry contains the following five sentences:
   I. Mr. Sands gave me a complete description of the robber.
   II. Alvin Sands, owner of the Star Delicatessen, called the precinct to report he had just been robbed.
   III. I then notified all police patrol vehicles to look for a white male in his early twenties wearing brown pants and shirt, a black leather jacket, and black and white sneakers.
   IV. I arrived on the scene after being notified by the precinct that a robbery had just occurred at the Star Delicatessen.
   V. Twenty minutes later, a man fitting the description was arrested by a police officer on patrol six blocks from the delicatessen.
   The MOST logical order for the above sentences to appear in the Activity Log is
   A. II, I, IV, III, V   B. II IV, III, I, V   C. II, IV, I, III, V   D. II, IV, I, V, III

2.____

3. Police Officer Benson is completing a Complaint Report concerning a stolen taxicab, which will include the following five sentences:
   I. Police Officer Benson noticed that a cab was parked next to a fire hydrant.
   II. Dawson *borrowed* the cab for transportation purposes since he was in a hurry.
   III. Ed Dawson got into his car and tried to start it, but the battery was dead.
   IV. When he reached his destination, he parked the cab by a fire hydrant and placed the keys under the seat.
   V. He looked around and saw an empty cab with the engine running.
   The MOST logical order for the above sentences to appear in the report is
   A. I, III, II, IV, V   B. III, I, II, V, IV   C. III, V, II, IV, I   D. V, II, IV, III, I

3.____

133

4. Police Officer Hatfield is reviewing his Activity Log entry prior to completing a report. The entry contains the following five sentences:
   I. When I arrived at Zand's Jewelry Store, I noticed that the door was slightly open.
   II. I told the burglar I was a police officer and that he should stand still or he would be shot.
   III. As I entered the store, I saw a man wearing a ski mask attempting to open the safe in the back of the store.
   IV. On December 16, 2020, at 1:38 A.M., I was informed that a burglary was in progress at Zand's Jewelry Store on East 59th Street.
   V. The burglar quickly pulled a knife from his pocket when he saw me.
   The MOST logical order for the above sentences to appear in the report is
   A. IV, I, III, V, II   B. I, IV, III, V, II   C. IV, III, II, V, I   D. I, III, IV, V, II

5. Police Officer Lorenz is completing a report of a murder. The report will contain the following five statements made by a witness:
   I. I was awakened by the sound of a gunshot coming from the apartment next door and I decided to check.
   II. I entered the apartment and looked into the kitchen and the bathroom.
   III. I found Mr. Hubbard's body slumped in the bathtub.
   IV. The door to the apartment was open, but I didn't see anyone.
   V. He had been shot in the head.
   The MOST logical order for the above sentences to appear in the report is
   A. I, III, II, IV, V   B. I, IV, II, III, V   C. IV, II, I, III, V   D. III, I, II, IV, V

6. Police Officer Baldwin is preparing an accident report which will include the following five sentences:
   I. The old man lay on the ground for a few minutes, but was not physically hurt.
   II. Charlie Watson, a construction worker, was repairing some brick work at the top of a building at 54th Street and Madison Avenue.
   III. Steven Green, his partner, warned him that this could be dangerous, but Watson ignored him.
   IV. A few minutes later, one of the bricks thrown by Watson smashed to the ground in front of an old man, who fainted out of fright.
   V. Mr. Watson began throwing some of the bricks over the side of the building.
   The MOST logical order for the above sentences to appear in the report is
   A. II, V, III, IV, I   B. I, IV, II, V, III   C. III, II, IV, V, I   D. II, III, I, IV, V

7. Police Officer Porter is completing an Incident Report concerning her rescue of a woman being held hostage by a former boyfriend. Her report will contain the following five sentences:
   I. I saw a man holding .25 caliber gun to a woman's head, but he did not see me.
   II. I then broke a window and gained access to the house.
   III. As I approached the house on foot, a gunshot rang out and I heard a woman scream.
   IV. A decoy van brought me as close as possible to the house where the woman was being held hostage.

V. I ordered the man to drop his gun, and he released the woman and was taken into custody.
The MOST logical order for the above sentences to appear in the report is
A. I, III, II, IV, V   B. IV, III, II, I, V   C. III, II, I, IV, V   D. V, I, II, III, IV

8. Police Officer Byrnes is preparing a crime report concerning a robbery. The report will consist of the following five sentences:
   I. Mr. White, following the man's instructions, opened the car's hood, at which time the man got out of the auto, drew a revolver, and ordered White to give him all the money in his pockets.
   II. Investigation has determined there were no witnesses to this incident.
   III. The man asked White to check the oil and fill the tank.
   IV. Mr. White, a gas attendant, states that he was working alone at the gas station when a black male pulled up to the gas pump in a white Mercury.
   V. White was then bound and gagged by the male and locked in the gas station's rest room.
   The MOST logical order for the above sentences to appear in the report is
   A. IV, I, III, II, V   B. III, I, II, V, IV   C. IV, III, I, V, II   D. I, III, IV, II, V

9. Police Officer Gale is preparing a report of a crime committed against Mr. Weston. The report will consist of the following five sentences:
   I. The man, who had a gun, told Mr. Weston not to scream for help and ordered him back into the apartment.
   II. With Mr. Weston disposed of in this fashion, the man proceeded to ransack the apartment.
   III. Opening the door to see who was there, Mr. Weston was confronted by a tall white male wearing a dark blue jacket and white pants.
   IV. Mr. Weston was at home alone in his living room when the doorbell rang.
   V. Once inside, the man bound and gagged Mr. Weston and locked him in the bathroom.
   The MOST logical order for the above sentences to appear in the report is
   A. III, V, II, I, IV   B. IV, III, I, V, II   C. III, V, IV, II, I   D. IV, III, V, I, II

10. A police officer is completing a report of a robbery, which will contain the following five sentences:
    I. Two police officers were about to enter the Red Rose Coffee Shop on 47th Street and 8th Avenue.
    II. They then noticed a male running up the street carrying a brown paper bag.
    III. They heard a woman standing outside the Broadway Boutique yelling that her store had just been robbed by a young man, and she was pointing up the street.
    IV. They caught up with him and made an arrest.
    V. The police officers pursued the male, who ran past them on 8th Avenue.
    The MOST logical order for the above sentences to appear in the report is
    A. I, III, II, V, IV   B. III, I, II, V, IV   C. IV, V, I, II, III   D. I, V, IV, III, II

11. Police Officer Capalbo is preparing a report of a bank robbery. The report will contain the following five statements made by a witness:
    I. Initialing, all I could see were two men, dressed in maintenance uniforms, sitting in the area reserved for bank officers.
    II. I was passing the bank at 8 P.M. and noticed that all the lights were out, except in the rear section.
    III. Then I noticed two other men in the bank, coming from the direction of the vault, carrying a large metal box.
    IV. At this point, I decided to call the police.
    V. I knocked on the window to get the attention of the men in the maintenance uniforms, and they chased the two men carrying the box down a flight of steps.
    The MOST logical order for the above sentences to appear in the report is
    A. IV, I, II, V, III B. I, III, II, V, IV C. II, I, III, V, IV D. II, III, I, V, IV

11._____

12. Police Officer Roberts is preparing a crime report concerning an assault and a stolen car. The report will contain the following five sentences:
    I. Upon leaving the store to return to his car, Winters noticed that a male unknown to him was sitting in his car.
    II. The man then re-entered Winters' car and drove away, fleeing north on 2nd Avenue.
    III. Mr. Winters stated that he parked his car in front of 235 East 25th Street and left the engine running while he went into the butcher shop at that location.
    IV. Mr. Robert Gering, a witness, stated that the male is known in the neighborhood as Bobby Rae and is believed to reside at 323 East 114th Street.
    V. When Winters approached the car and ordered the man to get out, the man got out of the auto and struck Winters with his fists, knocking him to the ground.
    The MOST logical order for the above sentences to appear in the report is
    A. III, II, V, I, IV B. III, I, V, II, IV C. I, IV, V, II, III D. III, II, I, V, IV

12._____

13. Police Officer Robinson is preparing a crime report concerning the robbery of Mr. Edwards' store. The report will consist of the following five sentences:
    I. When the last customer left the store, the two men drew revolvers and ordered Mr. Edwards to give them all the money in the cash register.
    II. The men proceeded to the back of the store as if they were going to do some shopping.
    III. Janet Morley, a neighborhood resident, later reported that she saw the men enter a green Ford station wagon and flee northbound on Albany Avenue.
    IV. Edwards complied after which the gunmen ran from the store.
    V. Mr. Edwards states that he was stocking merchandise behind the store counter when two white males entered the store.
    The MOST logical order for the above sentences to appear in the report is
    A. V, II, III, I, IV B. V, II, I, IV, III C. II, I, V, IV, III D. III, V, II, I, IV

13._____

14. Police Officer Wendell is preparing an accident report for a 6-car accident that occurred at the intersection of Bath Avenue and Bay Parkway. The report will consist of the following five sentences:
    I. A 2016 Volkswagen Beetle, traveling east on Bath Avenue, swerved to the left to avoid the Impala, and struck a 2014 Ford station wagon which was traveling west on Bath Avenue.
    II. The Seville then mounted the curb on the northeast corner of Bath Avenue and Bay Parkway and struck a light pole.
    III. A 2013 Buick Lesabre, traveling northbound on Bay Parkway directly behind the Impala, struck the Impala, pushing it into the intersection of Bath Avenue and Bay Parkway.
    IV. A 2015 Chevy Impala, traveling northbound on Bay Parkway, had stopped for a red light at Bath Avenue.
    V. A 2017 Toyota, traveling westbound on Bath Avenue, swerved to the right to avoid hitting the Ford station wagon, and struck a 2017 Cadillac Seville double-parked near the corner.
    The MOST logical order for the above sentences to appear in the report is
    A. IV, III, V, II, I   B. III, IV, V, II, I   C. IV, III, I, V, II   D. III, IV, V, I, II

15. The following five sentences are part of an Activity Log entry Police Officer Rogers made regarding an explosion:
    I. I quickly treated the pedestrian for the injury.
    II. The explosion caused a glass window in an office building to shatter.
    III. After the pedestrian was treated, a call was placed to the precinct requesting additional police officers to evacuate the area.
    IV. After all the glass settled to the ground, I saw a pedestrian who was bleeding from the arm.
    V. While on foot patrol near 5th Avenue and 53rd Street, I heard a loud explosion.
    The MOST logical order for the above sentences to appear in the report is
    A. II, V, IV, I, III   B. V, II, IV, III, I   C. V, II, I, IV, III   D. V, II, IV, I, III

16. Police Officer David is completing a report regarding illegal activity near the entrance to Madison Square Garden during a recent rock concert. The report will obtain the following five sentences:
    I. As I came closer to the man, he placed what appeared to be tickets in his pocket and began to walk away.
    II. After the man stopped, I questioned him about *scalping* tickets.
    III. While on assignment near the Madison Square Garden entrance, I observed a man apparently selling tickets.
    IV. I stopped the man by stating that I was a police officer.
    V. The man was then given a summons, and he left the area.
    The MOST logical order for the above sentences to appear in the report is
    A. I, III, IV, II, V   B. III, I, IV, V, II   C. III, IV, I, II, V   D. III, I, IV, II, V

17. Police Officer Sampson is preparing a report containing a dispute in a bar. The report will contain the following five sentences:
   I. John Evans, the bartender, ordered the two men out of the bar.
   II. Two men dressed in dungarees entered the C and D Bar at 5:30 P.M.
   III. The two men refused to leave and began to beat up Evans.
   IV. A customer in the bar saw me on patrol and yelled to me to come separate the three men.
   V. The two men became very drunk and loud within a short time.
   The MOST logical order for the above sentences to appear in the report is
   A. II, I, V, III, IV   B. II, III, IV, V, I   C. III, I, II, V, IV   D. II, V, I, III, IV

18. A police officer is completing a report concerning the response to a crime in progress. The report will include the following five sentences:
   I. The officers saw two armed men run out of the liquor store and into a waiting car.
   II. Police Officers Lunty and Duren received the call and responded to the liquor store.
   III. The robbers gave up without a struggle.
   IV. Lunty and Duren blocked the getaway car with their patrol car.
   V. A call came into the precinct concerning a robbery in progress at Jane's Liquor Store.
   The MOST logical order for the above sentence to appear in the report is
   A. V, II, I, IV, III   B. II, V, I, III, IV   C. V, I, IV, II, III   D. I, V, II, III, IV

19. Police Officers Jenkins is preparing a Crime Report which will consist of the following five sentences:
   I. After making inquirie in the vicinity, Smith found out that his next door neighbor, Viola Jones, had seen two local teenagers, Michael Heinz and Vincent Gaynor, smash his car's windshields with a crowbar.
   II. Jones told Smith that the teenagers live at 8700 19th Avenue.
   III. Mr. Smith heard a loud crash at approximately 11:00 P.M., looked out of his apartment window, and saw two white males running away from his car.
   IV. Smith then reported the incident to the precinct, and Heinz and Gaynor were arrested at the address given.
   V. Leaving his apartment to investigate further, Smith discovered that his car's front and rear windshields had been smashed.
   The MOST logical order for the above sentences to appear in the report is
   A. III, IV, V, I, II   B. III, V, I, II, IV   C. III, I, V, II, IV   D. V, III, I, II, IV

20. Sergeant Nancy Winston is reviewing a Gun Control Report which will contain the following five sentences:
   I. The man fell to the floor when hit in the chest with three bullets from 22 caliber gun.
   II. Merriam's 22 caliber gun was seized, and he was given a summons for not having a pistol permit.
   III. Christopher Merriam, the owner of A-Z Grocery, shot a man who attempted to rob him.
   IV. Police Officer Franks responded and asked Merriam for his pistol permit, which he could not produce.

V. Merriam phoned the police to report he had just shot a man who had attempted to rob him.

The MOST logical order for the above sentences to appear in the report is
   A. III, I, V, IV, II   B. I, III, V, IV, II   C. III, I, V, II, IV   D. I, III, II, V, IV

21. Detective John Manville is completing a report for his superior regarding the murder of an unknown male who was shot in Central Park. The report will contain the following five sentences:
   I. Police Officers Langston and Cavers responded to the scene.
   II. I received the assignment to investigate the murder in Central Park from Detective Sergeant Rogers.
   III. Langston notified the Detective Bureau after questioning Jason.
   IV. An unknown male, apparently murdered, was discovered in Central Park by Howard Jason, a park employee, who immediately called the police.
   V. Langston and Cavers questioned Jason.

The MOST logical order for the above sentences to appear in the report is
   A. I, IV, V, III, II   B. IV, I, V, II, III   C. IV, I, V, III, II   D. IV, V, I, III, II

22. A police officer is completing a report concerning the arrest of a juvenile. The report will contain the following five sentences:
   I. Sanders then telephoned Jay's parents from the precinct to inform them of their son's arrest.
   II. The store owner resisted, and Jay then shot him and ran from the store.
   III. Jay was transported directly to the precinct by Officer Sanders.
   IV. James Jay, a juvenile, walked into a candy store and announced a hold-up.
   V. Police Officer Sanders, while on patrol, arrested Jay a block from the candy store.

The MOST logical order for the above sentences to appear in the report is
   A. IV, V, II, I, III   B. IV, II, V, III, I   C. II, IV, V, III, I   D. V, IV, II, I, III

23. Police Officer Olsen prepared a crime report for a robbery which contained the following five sentences:
   I. Mr. Gordon was approached by this individual who then produced a gun and demanded the money from the cash register.
   II. The man then fled from the scene on foot, southbound on 5th Avenue.
   III. Mr. Gordon was working at the deli counter when a white male, 5'6", 150-160 lbs., wearing a green jacket and blue pants, entered the store.
   IV. Mr. Gordon complied with the man's demands and handed him the daily receipts.
   V. Further investigation has determined there are no other witnesses to this robbery.

The MOST logical order for the above sentences to appear in the report is
   A. I, III, IV, V, II   B. I, IV, II, III, V   C. III, IV, I, V, II   D. III, I, IV, II, V

24. Police Officer Bryant responded to 285 E. 31st Street to take a crime report of a burglary of Mr. Bond's home. The report will contain a brief description of the incident, consisting of the following five sentences:
   I. When Mr. Bond attempted to stop the burglar by grabbing him, he was pushed to the floor.
   II. The burglar had apparently gained access to the home by forcing open the 2nd floor bedroom window facing the fire escape.
   III. Mr. Bond sustained a head injury in the scuffle, and the burglar exited the home through the front door.
   IV. Finding nothing in the dresser, the burglar proceeded downstairs to the first floor, where he was confronted by Mr. Bond who was reading in the dining room.
   V. Once inside, he searched the drawers of the bedroom dresser.
   The MOST logical order for the above sentences to appear in the report is
   A. V, IV, I, II, III   B. II, V, IV, I, III   C. II, IV, V, III, I   D. III, II, I, V, IV

25. Police Officer Derringer responded to a call of a rape-homicide case in his patrol area and was ordered to prepare an incident report, which will contain the following five sentences:
   I. He pushed Miss Scott to the ground and forcibly raped her.
   II. Mary Scott was approached from behind by a white male, 5'7", 150-160 lbs. wearing dark pants and a white jacket.
   III. As Robinson approached the male, he ordered him to stop.
   IV. Screaming for help, Miss Scott alerted one John Robinson, a local grocer, who chased her assailant as he fled the scene.
   V. The male turned and fired two shots at Robinson, who fell to the ground mortally wounded.
   The MOST logical order for the above sentences to appear in the report is
   A. IV, III, I, II, V   B. II, IV, III, V, I   C. II, IV, I, V, III   D. II, I, IV, III, V

KEY (CORRECT ANSWERS)

1.	B		11.	C
2.	C		12.	B
3.	C		13.	B
4.	A		14.	C
5.	B		15.	D
6.	A		16.	D
7.	B		17.	D
8.	C		18.	A
9.	B		19.	B
10.	A		20.	A

21. C
22. B
23. D
24. B
25. D

BASIC FUNDAMENTALS OF FINGERPRINT SCIENCE

I. IMPORTANCE OF FINGERPRINTS AS PHYSICAL EVIDENCE

Fingerprints are perhaps the most common form of physical evidence, and certainly one of the most valuable. They relate directly to the ultimate objective of every criminal investigation--the identification of the offender.

Fingerprints of the offender are frequently found at the scene of a crime, and they may take more than one form. However, in all cases, the prints are fragile and susceptible to complete destruction by the first careless act. They are also, in many cases, difficult to find. This chapter discusses the basic requirements for conducting a successful search for fingerprints, together with the means of recognizing, lifting, and preserving them for later analysis.

With but a few exceptions, everyone has fingerprints. This universal character is a prime factor in the establishment of a standard of identification. Since a print of one finger has never been known to exactly duplicate another fingerprint (even of the same person or identical twin) it is possible to identify an individual with just one impression. The relative ease with which a set of <u>inked</u> fingerprints can be taken as a means of identification is a further basis for using this standard. Despite such factors as aging and a variety of environmental influences, a person's fingerprints have never been known to change. The unchanging pattern thus provides a permanent record of the individual throughout life.

Although there are many different filing systems for fingerprints, each is based on classification of common characteristics. The classification system works to readily categorize a set of fingerprints, as well as to provide quick access to a set of prints with a given characteristic.

II. DEFINITION OF FINGERPRINTS

A direct or inked fingerprint is an impression of the ridge detail of the underside of the fingers, palms, toes, or the soles of the feet. This is contrasted with a latent print, which is an impression caused by the perspiration through the sweat pores on the ridges of the skin being transferred to some surface. Fingerprints also occur as residues when the finger ridges have been contaminated with such materials as oil, dirt, blood, and grease.

III. BASIS OF IDENTIFICATION OF FINGERPRINTS

The ridge detail of fingerprints including ends of ridges, their separations, and their relationship to each other constitute the basis for identification of fingerprints. The basic points of comparison of prints are shown in Figure 1. In checking for similarity, most experts require from 10 to 12 points although there is no specific number required. However, regardless of the points of similarity, should an unexplainable difference appear, positive identification cannot be made.

There is no set print size requirement for positive identification. The only requirement is that the print be large enough to contain at least 10 to 12 points. This requirement count may be met by an area as small as the end of a pencil. As a general rule, if the investigator develops an area which appears to have several ridges, regardless of the size of the area, it should be lifted, marked, and submitted to the laboratory.

Some investigators believe that the points used for identification of the fingerprint occur only in the pattern area of the finger. This is not true. All the different types occur outside of the pattern area on the finger as well as on the first and second joint of the finger and the entire palm of the hand. They are also present on the toes and the entire sole of the foot. In fact, they may be found in any area where friction ridges occur.

IV. LIMITATIONS OF LATENT PRINTS

Even though latent prints are invaluable in the course of investigative work, there are certain limitations as to what information these prints can be expected to provide. It is impossible, for example, to determine the age of the latent print because there are a number of factors other than time that change the appearance of the developed latent. It is sometimes possible, however, to estimate the age of the print in relation to certain events. For example, prints appearing on an object thoroughly cleaned during a recent housecleaning can be dated as occurring after that event.

Likewise, it is not possible to determine, from the examination of the print alone, the age or sex of the person leaving the print. Even though a rough correlation does exist between age and sex and such characteristics as size of the ridge or pattern, individual variations occur.

BASIC FINGERPRINT COMPARISONS

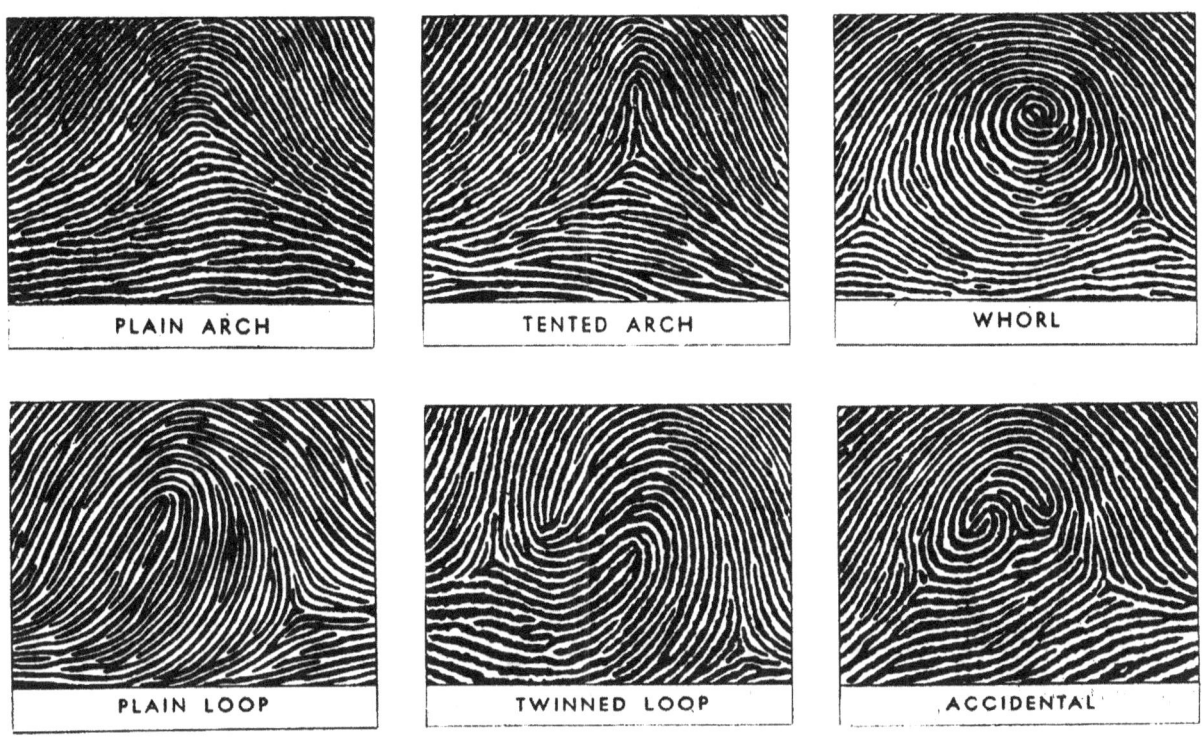

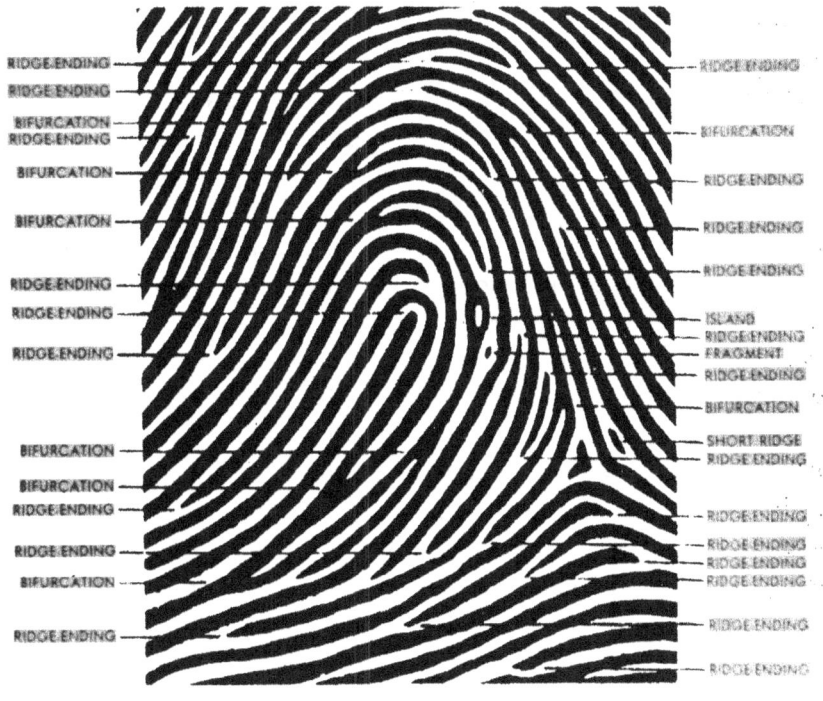

FIGURE 1

Prints cannot be used to identify the race of a suspect, nor can occupational groups be determined with an accepted degree of accuracy on the basis of fingerprints. It is true that many occupations, such as bricklaying, cause certain characteristic damage to the skin of the fingers and hands. However, any conjecture as to occupation of a suspect made on this basis should be considered only as an investigative lead and not as substantive evidence.

V. CONDITIONS WHICH AFFECT LATENT PRINTS

The quality of latent fingerprints is affected by such conditions as the type of surface material, the manner in which the print was transferred, nature and quantity of the substance (perspiration, oils, blood, etc.) which covered the ridge surfaces, weather conditions, and, to some extent, the physical or occupational defects of the person transferring the print. The processing of prints as it relates to these conditions is discussed later under "METHOD OF DEVELOPING FINGERPRINTS."

The nature and the condition of the surface on which the latent print is deposited are very important. The surface must be fairly clean and smooth or the ridge detail of the finger will be lost. Such surfaces as coarse cloth, unfinished wood, grained leather, etc., are very poor surfaces for fingerprints.

Another important consideration is the manner in which the object was touched or released. The ridges on fingers are very close together. Should the finger move just the distance between two ridges when touching or releasing an object, most of the ridge detail will be lost. This condition explains why most latents which are developed are smeared in the pattern area and only their ridges outside the pattern area have enough detail for identification.

There are conditions which occur that cause the friction surfaces to become completely covered with perspiration or other materials. When such materials cover not only the ridge surface of the skin, but fill the valleys as well, no ridge detail can be recorded. Prints of this type generally develop very dark and appear about the same as a print that was developed with too much powder.

The weather affects the latent print in a number of ways. The print may be dried out or washed away. Humidity will cause latent prints on paper to become smudged or even disappear. Because of the sponge nature of paper, moisture enters it from all directions and causes the ridge detail to diffuse to the extent that it will not be recognized as a print.

The more oil that is deposited with perspiration, the longer the print will last. Since perspiration is mostly water, the oil that is deposited with it will float on the surface and reduce its evaporation rate. After the water evaporates, the oil remains and becomes quite tacky. This condition results in better development of the ridge detail when using fingerprint powder. Body oil is present on the friction ridges of the fingers as contamination from the hairy parts of the body and, therefore, may not be present in the latent print at all. When no oils are present, the water content of the deposited material is subject to the same evaporation rate as any like amount of water under the same conditions and the print will be less tacky.

VI. RESPONSIBILITY OF THE CRIME SCENE INVESTIGATOR IN COLLECTING FINGERPRINTS

Latent prints are such valuable evidence that extraordinary efforts should be made to recover them. The investigator is strongly urged to adopt a positive attitude toward this aspect of the search, regardless of any apparent problems.

It is absolutely imperative that the crime scene investigator make a thorough search of all surface areas in and around the scene of the crime that have the potential of retaining finger or palm prints. Particular attention should be paid to the less obvious places, such as the undersides of tiolet seats, table tops and dresser drawers, the surface of dinner plates, filing cabinets, the backs of chairs, rearview mirrors (both the glass and frame) and the trunk lids of automobiles. Heavily handled objects, such as door knobs or telephones, may not yield good prints. However, they are objects that are quite likely to be touched and should always be processed.

The investigator should not assume that the offender took precautions against leaving prints or that he destroyed those he did leave. A person committing a criminal offense is usually under some stress and may be prone to oversight. If he wore gloves he may have removed them for some operation, or they may have been torn.

It is helpful to attempt to view the scene as the criminal did. Hence, such conditions as time of day, weather, and physical layout may suggest that certain surface areas should be closely examined. In conducting the examination for latent prints in a burglary case, for example, it is suggested that the investigation begin at the point of entry. For other crimes, such as rape, the point of entry takes on less importance as a source of latent prints. Whatever the nature of the crime and the particular circumstances, its reconstruction by the investigator is intended to give practical direction to the search.

Valuable aid in obtaining latent print leads may be solicited from a person who is familiar with the usual physical layout of the crime scene, such as the owner of the building or the usual occupant of an apartment. That person should be allowed to observe at least a part of the preliminary investigation and be encouraged to point out items which appear out of place or to identify objects that may have been brought in by the suspect.

Things which have permanent serial numbers attached to them, such as automobiles, weapons, and machinery require special attention. In addition to checking such items for latent prints, it is good policy to make a lift of the serial number (using fingerprint tape), as well as prints and attach both to the same fingerprint card. Such direct lifts of serial numbers prove invaluable for latter reference, particularly as evidence in court.

VII. PRINTS WHICH REQUIRE NO FURTHER DEVELOPING

There are two basic types of latent prints that the crime scene examiner will likely encounter which do not need developing. The first of these is the visible type created after the suspect's hand has come in contact with blood, ink, paint, grease, dirt, etc., and the print transferred to some surface area. Prints made from these substances are usually distinct and should stand out to the investigator. The procedure to be used in collecting the print is to first photograph and then cover it with protective tape. The surface on which the print rests must then be transported to the crime laboratory. Common sense must rule the decision as to just how much damage is justifiable in collecting items or surface areas where prints are found.

The second type of print which requires no further developing is an impression in a soft substance such as putty, clay, or fresh paint. Again, the procedure is to first photograph the impression, then transport the object or a section containing it to the crime laboratory. If a physical transfer of the impression is not possible, it should be sprayed with shellac and a cast prepared of silicone rubber. The cast should then be identified and sent to the laboratory in place of the actual imprint.

VIII. METHOD OF DEVELOPING FINGERPRINTS

The types of surfaces from which latent prints can be lifted fall into two broad categories: those which are hard, smooth, and nonabsorbent, and those which are smooth and absorbent. The crime scene investigator must be able to distinguish between these two types of surfaces because different procedures are used to develop latent prints on them.

Before developing the print, the fingerprint brush should be cleaned and the bristles separated. This is best done by rolling the handle rapidly between the palms of the hands and letting the bristles spread out naturally.

When the fingerprint powder is stored it tends to compact and becomes difficult to handle. Before opening the container it should be turned upside down and shaken vigorously to loosen the powder.

To determine in which category a given surface belongs, it is useful to think of what would happen to a drop of water if it were placed on it. If the water would bead up (as for example on plate glass) the surface is hard, smooth, and nonabsorbent. However, if the water would soak in, as on cardboard, the surface is absorbent.

IX. <u>Developing Prints on Nonabsorbent, Hard, Smooth Surfaces</u>

Prints made on nonabsorbent, hard materials will remain entirely on the surface of the object in the form of a delicate liquid or semisolid deposit. The print, mainly consisting of oil and water, expands upward from the surface which makes an ideal adhesive base for fingerprint powder.

The actual development process (illustrated in Figure 2) is begun by applying a small amount of fingerprint powder to the area to be examined, using the brush provided in the fingerprint kit. A <u>word of caution:</u> too much powder should not be used since an excessive amount will result in an overly darkened print in which points will be difficult to identify. The brush should just touch the powder, it is not necessary to bury it. The entire area to be processed should be covered using light, even strokes until some ridge detail begins to show. As the pattern of the ridges becomes visible the brush strokes should be directed to follow the contour lines. After all of the details of the print have been developed, the excess powder should be removed by gently brushing or blowing it away. The powder should be allowed to adhere to the wet, tacky area of the latent print but not to the surface on which the print is deposited. The print can be lifted by holding the folded or loose end of the tape with the thumb and the forefinger of one hand and the roll in the other, pulling out enough tape to cover the area to be lifted (usually about 5 or 6 inches), securing the loose end of the tape beside the print to be lifted and holding it there with the forefinger. Then the thumb should slide along the top of the tape forcing it gently down over the print. The roll, which is in the other hand, should not be released during this operation. The print is now protected. The powder used to develop the print is trapped between the tape and the surface of the object. Using care, the tape should be smoothed down over the print to force out all the air bubbles.

Once the tape has been secured, one of two procedures may be followed. If the surface would be destroyed by removing the tape, the tape may be left on and the entire object submitted to the laboratory for examination. If this is not practical, the print may be removed by pulling up on the roll end. When the tape is free of the surface, it is placed on a fingerprint card in the same manner as the tape was placed over the latent print. When the lift is secured to the card, the tape should be severed from the roll and the loose end folded up.

If the developed latent print is larger than the width of the tape, it still may be lifted by placing one strip beside another, allowing about 1/4 inch overlap with each additional strip until the desired area is covered.

METHOD OF DEVELOPING AND LIFTING LATENT FINGERPRINTS

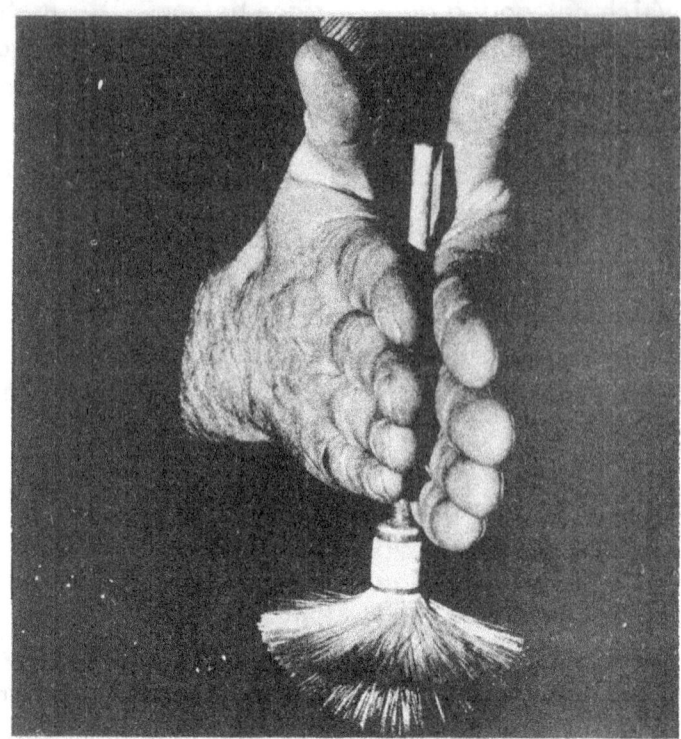

Fingerprint brush should be cleaned and bristles separated by rolling the brush handle rapidly between the hands.

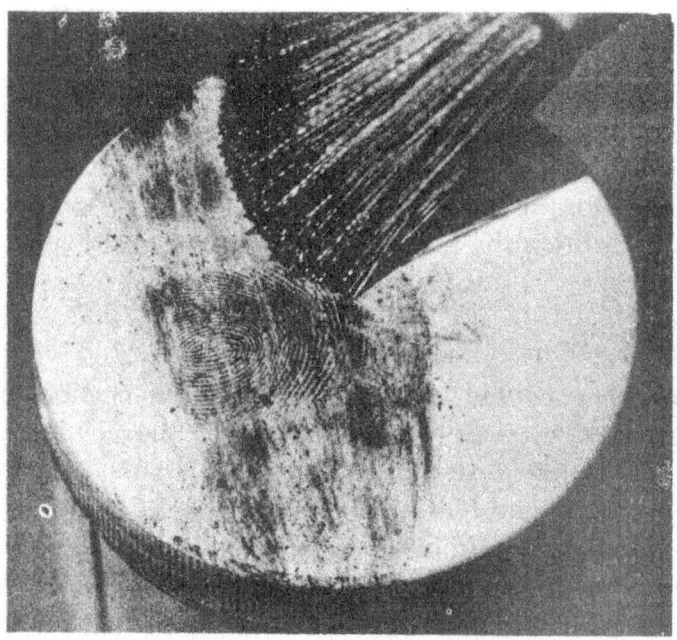

Applying powder to surface to discover the print.

FIGURE 2

METHOD OF DEVELOPING AND LIFTING LATENT FINGERPRINTS
(Continued)

Cleaning up the print by gently brushing with the flow of the ridges.

Proper method of starting to apply fingerprint tape.

FIGURE 2 (Continued)

METHOD OF DEVELOPING AND LIFTING LATENT FINGERPRINTS
(Concluded)

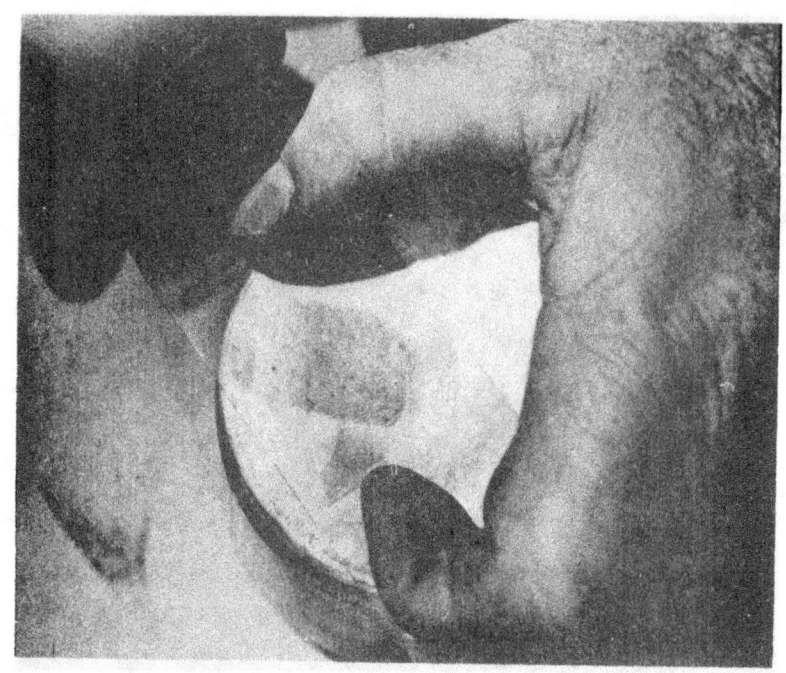

Tape is smoothed with thumb to remove air bubbles.

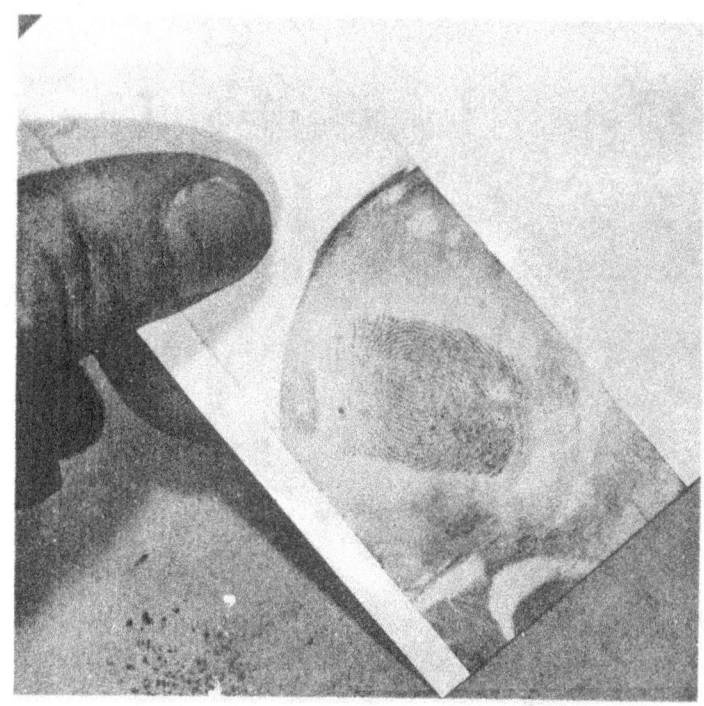

Lifted print is transferred to a fingerprint card.

FIGURE 2 (Concluded)

X. MARKING AND IDENTIFYING FINGERPRINT LIFTS

After a latent print has been developed, lifted, and placed on a card, it is necessary that the card be properly identified. Information recorded on the card should include the date, title of the case or number, address of the crime scene, name of the officer who made the lift, the exact place of the lift, and the type of object. If the card contains only one lift, the description of the exact place and the type of object lifted from may be placed on the back. If the card contains several lifts (which is permissible), then the exact place and the type object should be written on the front of the card close to the print. Regardless of how well the latent was developed and lifted, if the card is not properly marked with all the information legally required, and if the fingerprint specialist is not furnished with all the information and detail he requires, the whole effort is a waste of time.

In describing the exact place that the lift was made, it is sometimes convenient to draw a simple sketch of the object. This sketch should be made on the fingerprint card which is sent to the criminalistics laboratory. The inclusion of corresponding small arrows on both the lift and the sketch are also helpful in orienting the exact placement of a latent fingerprint.

If prints opposed to each other are lifted, as on both sides of a piece of broken glass, a notation of this fact should be made on the fingerprint card.

XI. COLLECTION OF ELIMINATION FINGERPRINTS

Before submitting lifted latent prints recovered from the crime scene to a fingerprint technician for examination, elimination prints of all persons who may have had access to the area should be made. With elimination prints, it is possible to exclude from the prints lifted all persons who had legal access to the crime scene.

Equipped with fingerprint ink, a glass plate, and a card holder, the investigator uses the following step-by-step procedure to obtain elimination fingerprints.

- The subject signs the fingerprint card.
- The officer signs and dates the same card.
- The subject washes his hands.
- The officer rolls ink over the surface of the inking slab.
- The officer instructs the subject to relax arm and hand muscles.
- The officer grasps the subject's hand, holds the four fingers back, and inks the thumb by rolling it toward the body. He immediately rolls the inked thumb in the designated space on the card and repeats the process for each of the fingers, rolling them away from the subject's body.

- To make simultaneous impressions, the prints are not rolled; rather the four fingers, extended and joined, are inked and the print is made by exerting a straight down pressure. The process is repeated for the thumbs (again no rolling).
- To make palm prints (needed only if palm prints were found at the crime scene), the entire palm and fingers are inked. The hand is then pressed straight down on a sequence card. A different card should be used for each hand.

If the glass plate and card holder are not available, the ink pad and the elimination cards furnished with the equipment may be used. In case of a homicide, the prints of the victim, including palm prints, must be obtained. The law requires positive identification of all murder victims. Both palm and finger prints are required as elimination prints.

If the investigating officer wishes to take elimination prints, and the equipment for taking inked prints is not available, he may use the same equipment he uses for developing latent prints. The subject's fingers are rolled on a card as though they were inked. After the card has been allowed to dry for a few minutes, the latent prints are dusted with fingerprint powder and when fully developed are covered with fingerprint tape. Both the subject and the officer should sign under a notation on the dated card that the prints are elimination prints.

BASIC FUNDAMENTALS OF TAKING PALM PRINTS

CONTENTS

	Page
INTRODUCTION	1
STEP 1 - Preparation of Inking Plate	2
STEP 2 - Preparation of Fingerprint Card	3
STEP 3 - Preparation of Subject's Palm	4
STEP 4 - Recording of Inked Impressions	5
STEP 5 - Completion of Fingerprint Card	8
CONCLUSION	12

BASIC FUNDAMENTALS OF TAKING PALM PRINTS

INTRODUCTION

The importance of using fingerprint evidence has been recognized by investigators and the courts for many years. Palmprint identifications are equally valuable as scientific investigative aids and proof of facts at subsequent trials. This is especially true in cases involving alleged forgeries, since a writer generally places the edge of his palm on the forged document when writing. The portion of the palm resting on the paper during the writing is often referred to as the "writers palm". The development of a "writers palmprint" on a document, if identical to a suspect's palmprint, provides strong evidence. Like fingerprints, however, maximum benefit from such evidence can only be achieved if inked or known palmprints are properly obtained.

The equipment necessary for taking inked palmprints has been furnished to each Secret Service field office. These materials are illustrated in Figure 1 on the next page. They consist of an inking plate, fingerprint ink (printer's black ink), ink roller, a metal cylinder and palmprint cards. If used correctly, proper recording of inked palmprints will be insured.

The steps to be followed in taking palmprint impressions are outlined on the following pages.

STEP 1 PREPARATION OF INKING PLATE

In order to obtain clear, legible palmprints, fingerprint ink must be spread on the inking plate in a thin, uniform coat. This can best be accomplished by placing a daub or two of ink on the plate. (Figure 2.) The ink can be spread evenly over the entire plate by rolling the ink roller back and forth over the plate until the desired consistency is obtained. (Figures 3 and 4.) The proper thickness of the ink may be judged by placing a slip of white paper under the inked glass plate. If the ink is of the desired thickness, the outline of the paper will be barely visible.

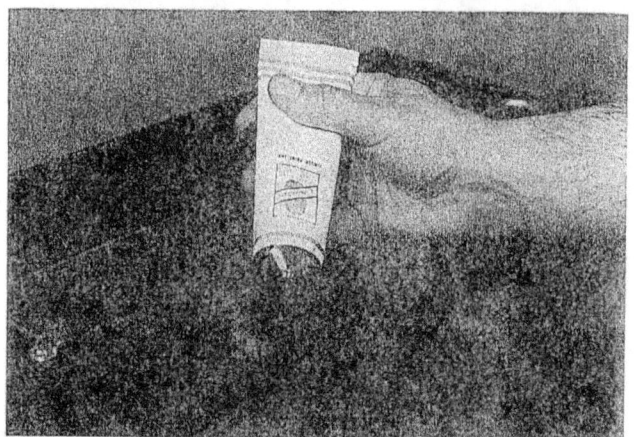

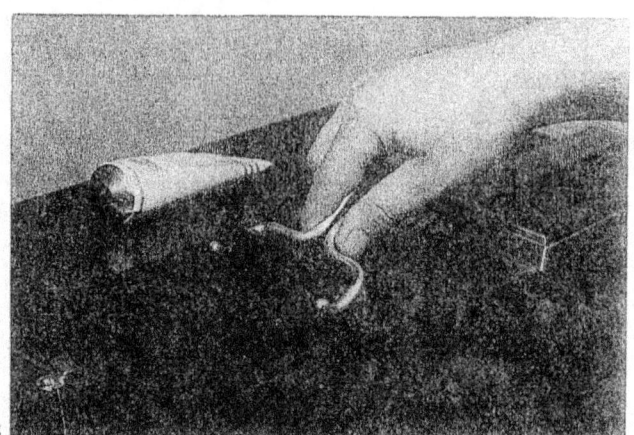

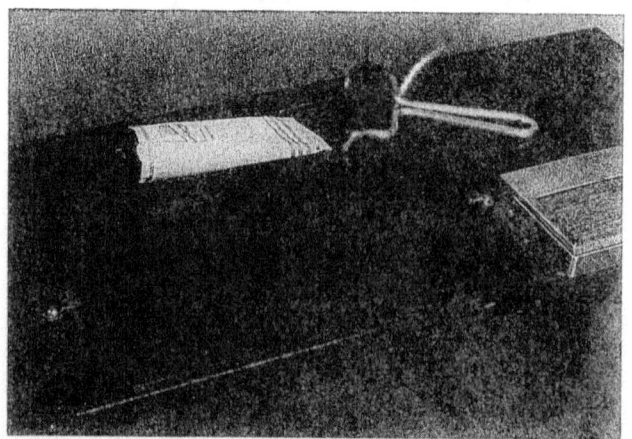

STEP 2: PREPARATION OF FINGERPRINT CARD

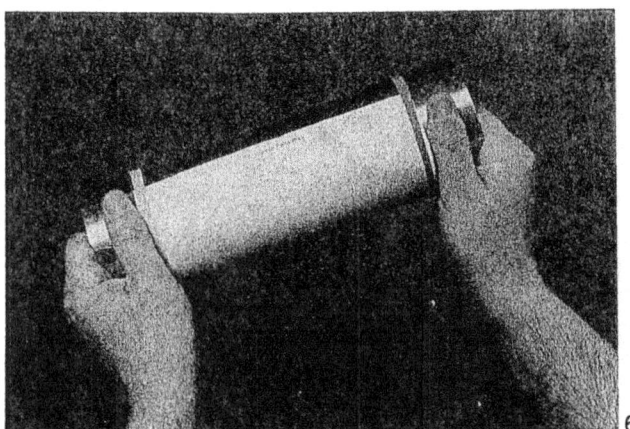

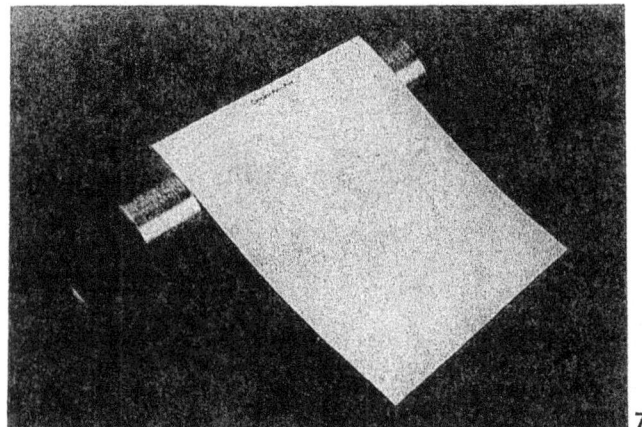

Having prepared the inking plate, the palmprint card, SSF 1793, should be secured to the palmprint roller (metal cylinder). The palmprint card is placed reverse side up to obtain the complete palmprint. (Figure 5.) When the card is wrapped around the cylinder it may be attached with rubber bands. (Figure 6.)

An alternate method which works equally well is to allow the card to "ride" the roller during the taking process. This method eliminates the need to secure the card to the roller. (Figure 7.) NOTE: The method used will vary with the individual preference of the technician or investigator taking the prints.

STEP 3 PREPARATION OF SUBJECT'S PALM

After the inking plate has been prepared and the palmprint card readied, the subject's palms should be inked. The areas of the individual's fingers and hands to be printed must be free of soil or other substances which could hinder the accurate recording of legible inked prints. Therefore, prior to inking, the subject's hand must be held in an open position and the entire palm area should be wiped clean. (Figure 8.)

The inking of the subject's hand is accomplished by, (1) rolling the ink roller over the inking plate to pick up a thin layer of ink (Figure 9) and, (2) transferring this ink to the palm by firmly rolling the ink roller on the hand, insuring an even deposit over the entire area. (Figure 10.)

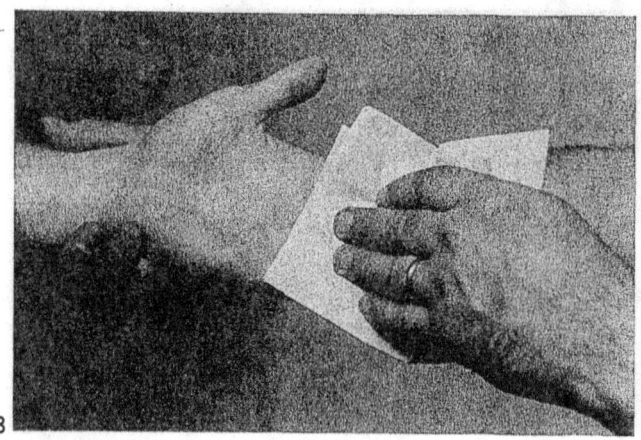
8

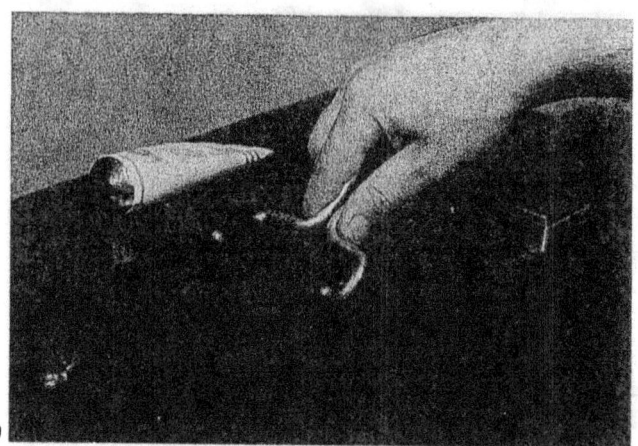
9

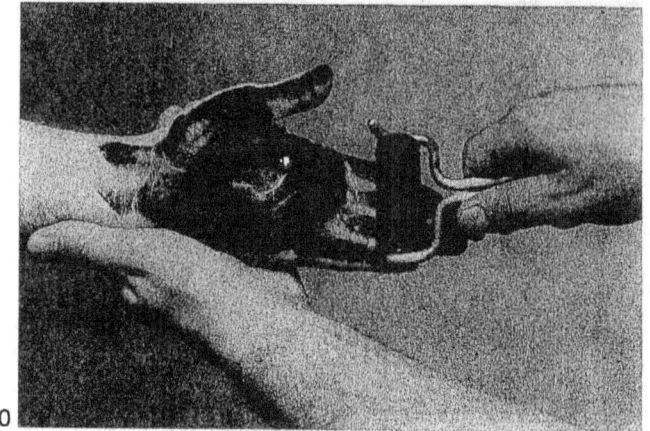
10

STEP 4 RECORDING OF INKED IMPRESSIONS

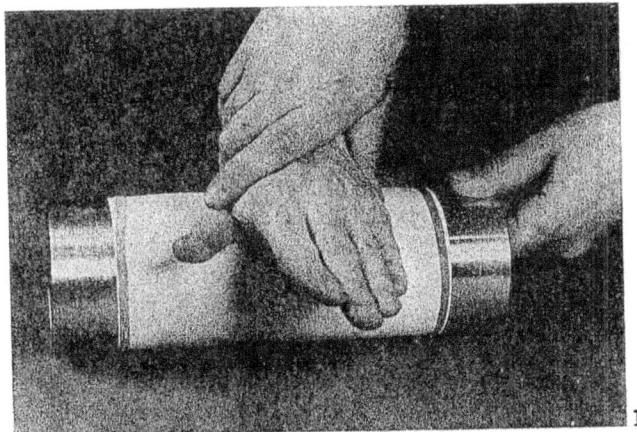
11

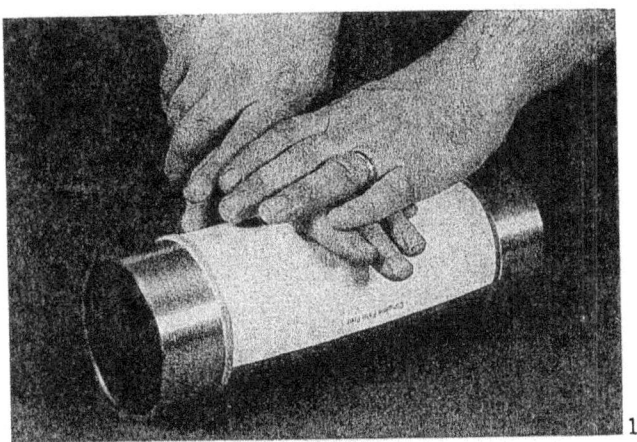
12

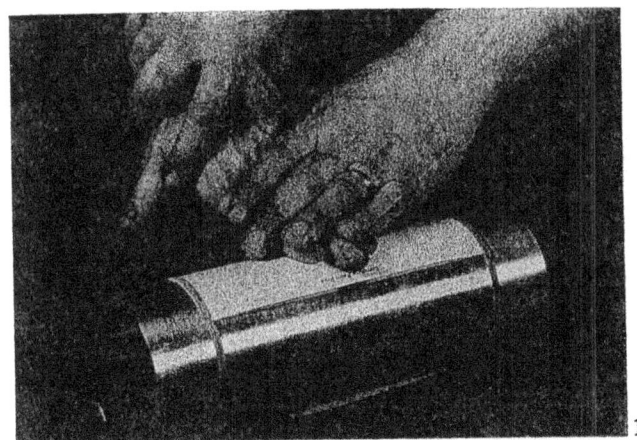
13

The next step is to record the entire palmprint on the palmprint card. The technician must guide and control the subject's hand throughout the recording. In order to facilitate the procedure, the metal cylinder with the fingerprint card should be situated so that it is slightly lower than the horizontal level of the subject's forearm.

The inked palm is now placed in contact with the palmprint card and the print is rolled onto the card. The print may be rolled toward or away from the subject. The direction of the roll is determined by the preference of the person taking the prints.

If the technician prefers to roll the print toward the subject, the heel of the palm is placed in contact with the bottom of the card and rolled toward the subject in a steady motion with firm even pressure being applied to the hand. (Figures 11, 12 and 13.)

If the technician prefers to roll the print away from the subject, the fingertips are placed in contact with the top of the card and rolled from the fingers to the heel of the hand. (Figures 14 and 15.) (Figures 14 and 15 also depict use of the card "riding" the roller rather than being held in place by rubber bands.)

While the direction of the rolling motion is a matter of choice, it should be remembered that once the roll has begun, it must be completed in one unceasing motion. Otherwise, print distortions or superimpositions may occur. The degree of pressure to be exerted in taking rolled palmprint impressions is also very important. The proper pressure may best be determined through experience and observation. Good, usable prints are those that are clearly legible and reveal all the minute ridge patterns and other details of the palm.

After obtaining a satisfactory rolled impression of the complete palm, it is necessary to take two rolled impressions of the sides of the subject's palms. These are the outside edges of the hand that rest on the paper or other surface when a person is writing, and are the "writers palms" referred to earlier. They are taken on the front of the palmprint card. To obtain these, the ink roller must be re-inked and the ink rolled evenly over the edge of the hand to be printed. (Figure 16.)

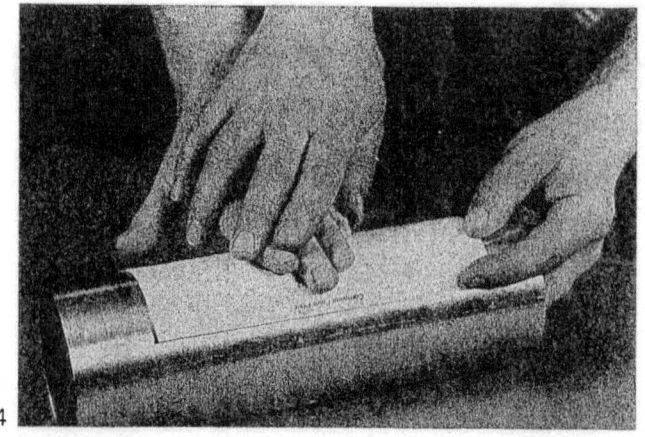

14

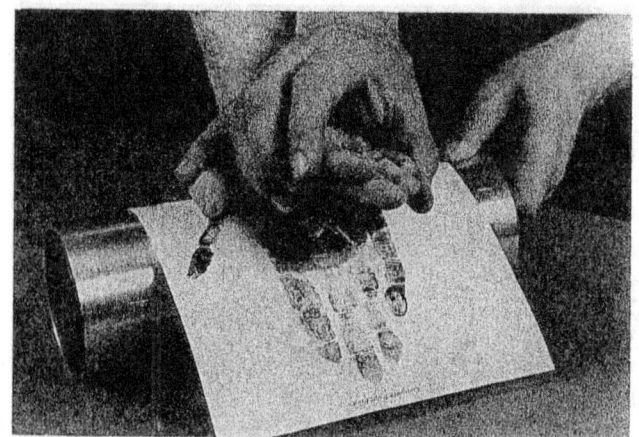

15

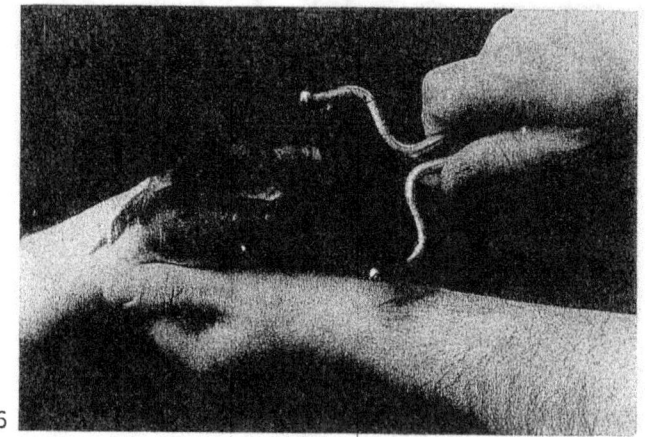

16

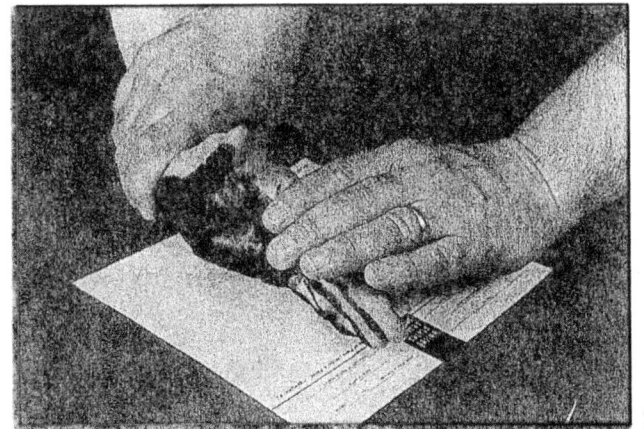

17

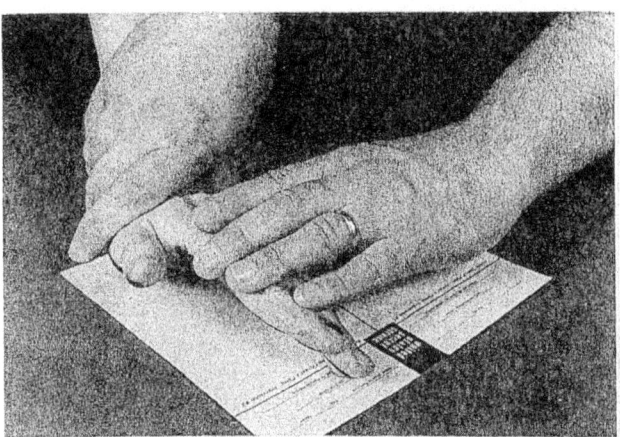

18

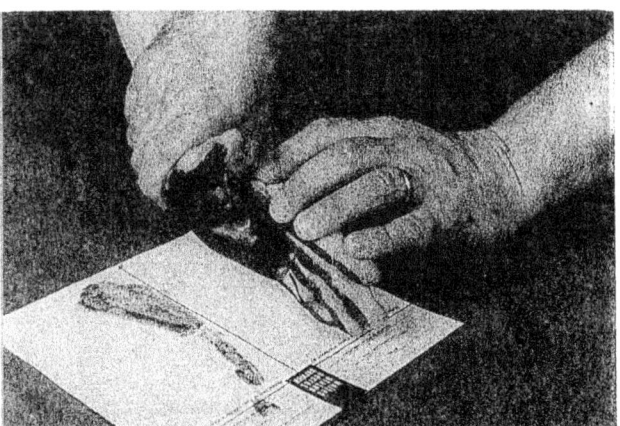

19

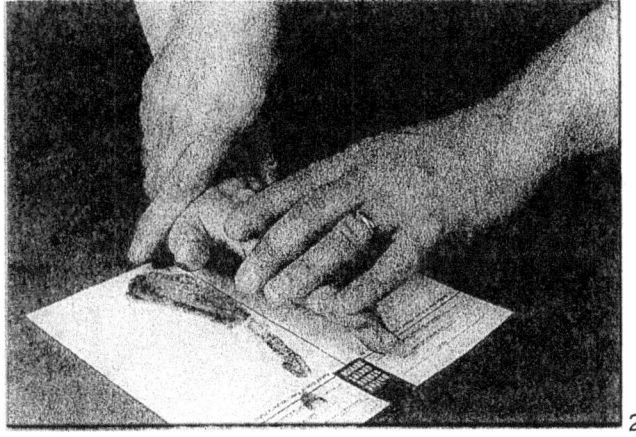

20

With the card lying on a flat surface, the inked palm is brought into firm direct contact with the card and rolled once from side to side to insure a complete recording of all identifiable ridges. (Figures 17 and 18.) If properly taken, the hairline on the outside of the hand should begin to appear.

The same "writers palm" should be recorded twice—once in the area on Form SSF 1793 marked "Impression No. 1" and again in the area marked "Impression No. 2". (Figures 19 and 20.) The hand should be freshly inked for each recording.

Each step must be repeated for both of the subject's hands, as at least one card for each palm is required.

STEP 5 COMPLETION OF FINGERPRINT CARD

Upon recording prints for both palms, the front of each card must be completed with

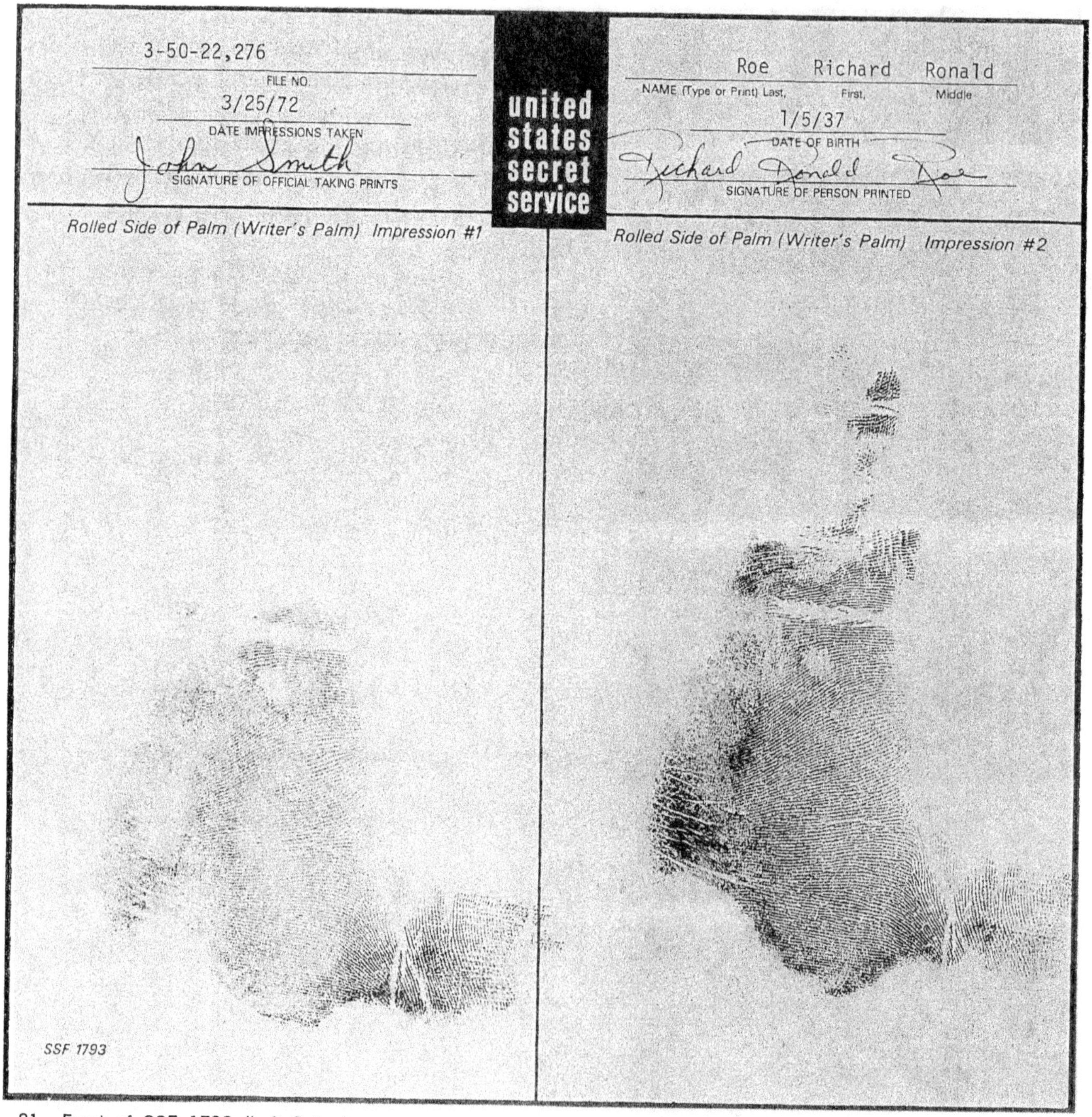

21 Front of SSF 1793 (Left Palm)

the information requested. The information should be typed or legibly printed. The signatures of the subject and the person taking the prints must be written. In furnishing the necessary information on the card, care should be taken not to smear the inked impressions. If the ink has not had time to dry sufficiently, a good practice to employ during

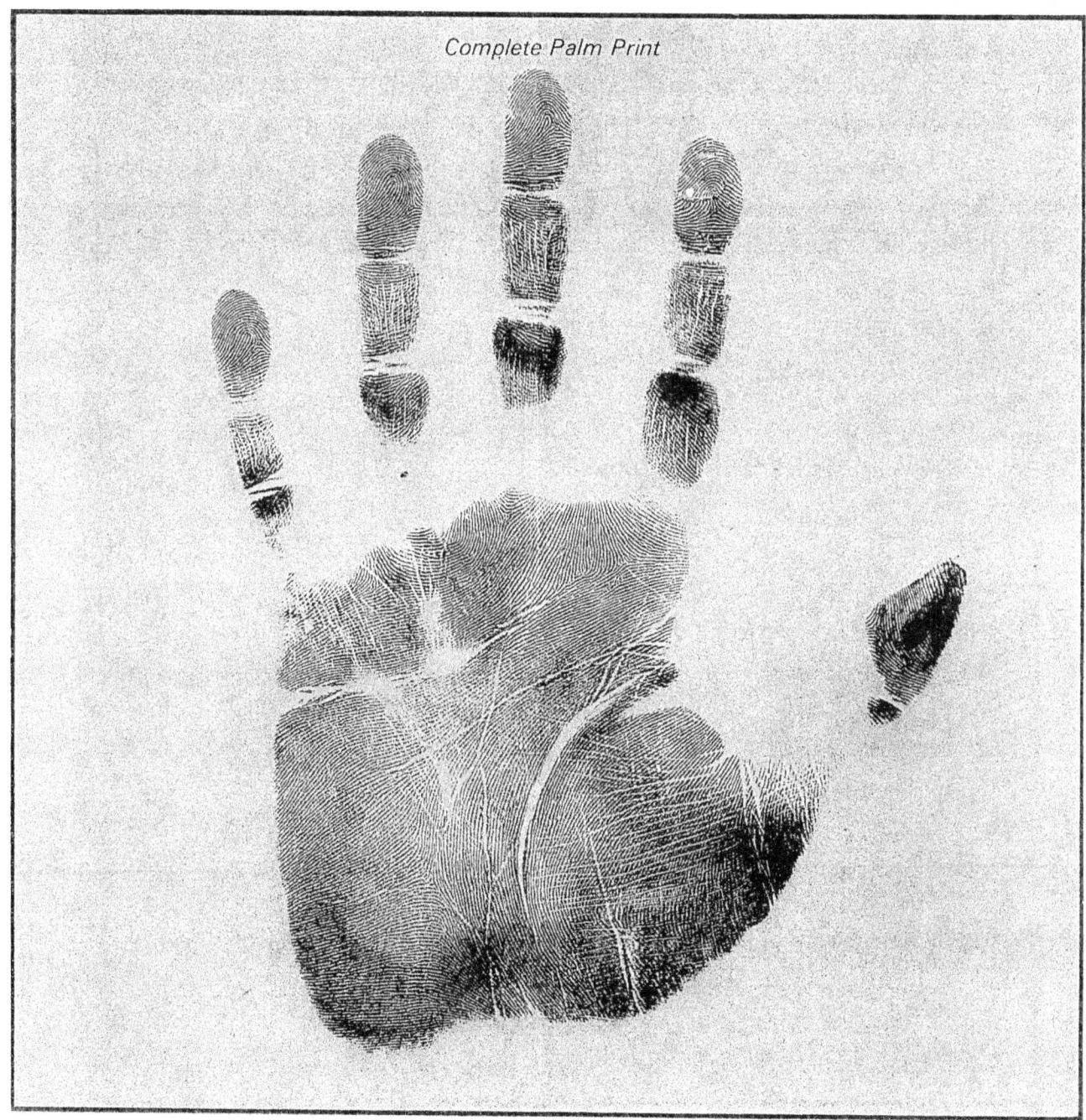

22 Back of SSF 1793 (Complete Left Palm)

the signing is to place a clean sheet of paper over the portion of the card containing the inked impressions so they will not be smudged.

Figures 21, 22, 23 and 24 represent properly completed palmprint cards. Two cards are needed. One card bears one complete palmprint and two impressions of the

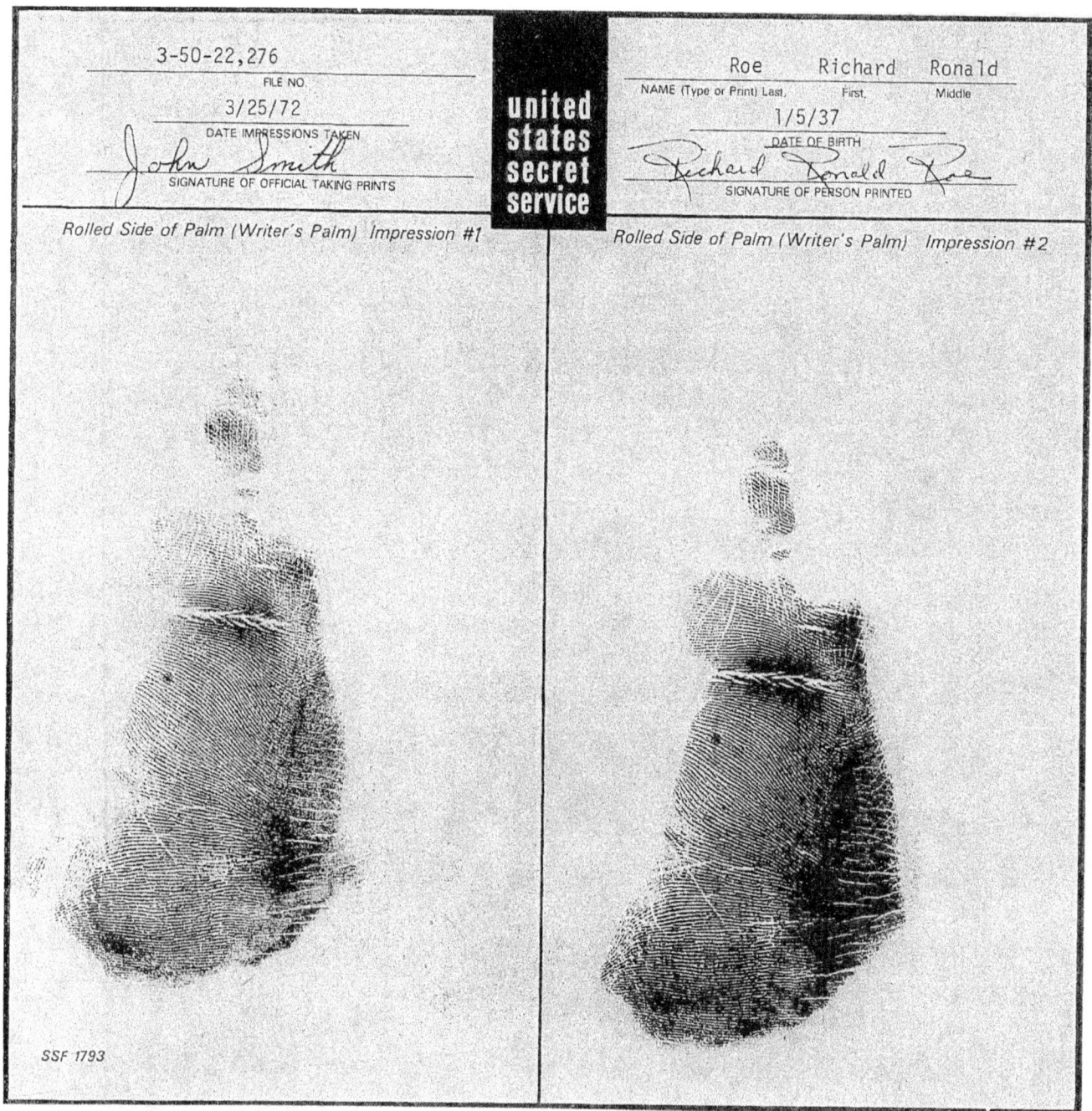

23   Front of SSF 1793 (Right Palm)

"writers palm" for the right hand and the second card contains similar prints of the left hand.

Both palmprint cards should be stapled to the subject's fingerprint card(s) so they will remain together. Stapling should be at the top center edge of the cards away from areas bearing inked prints.

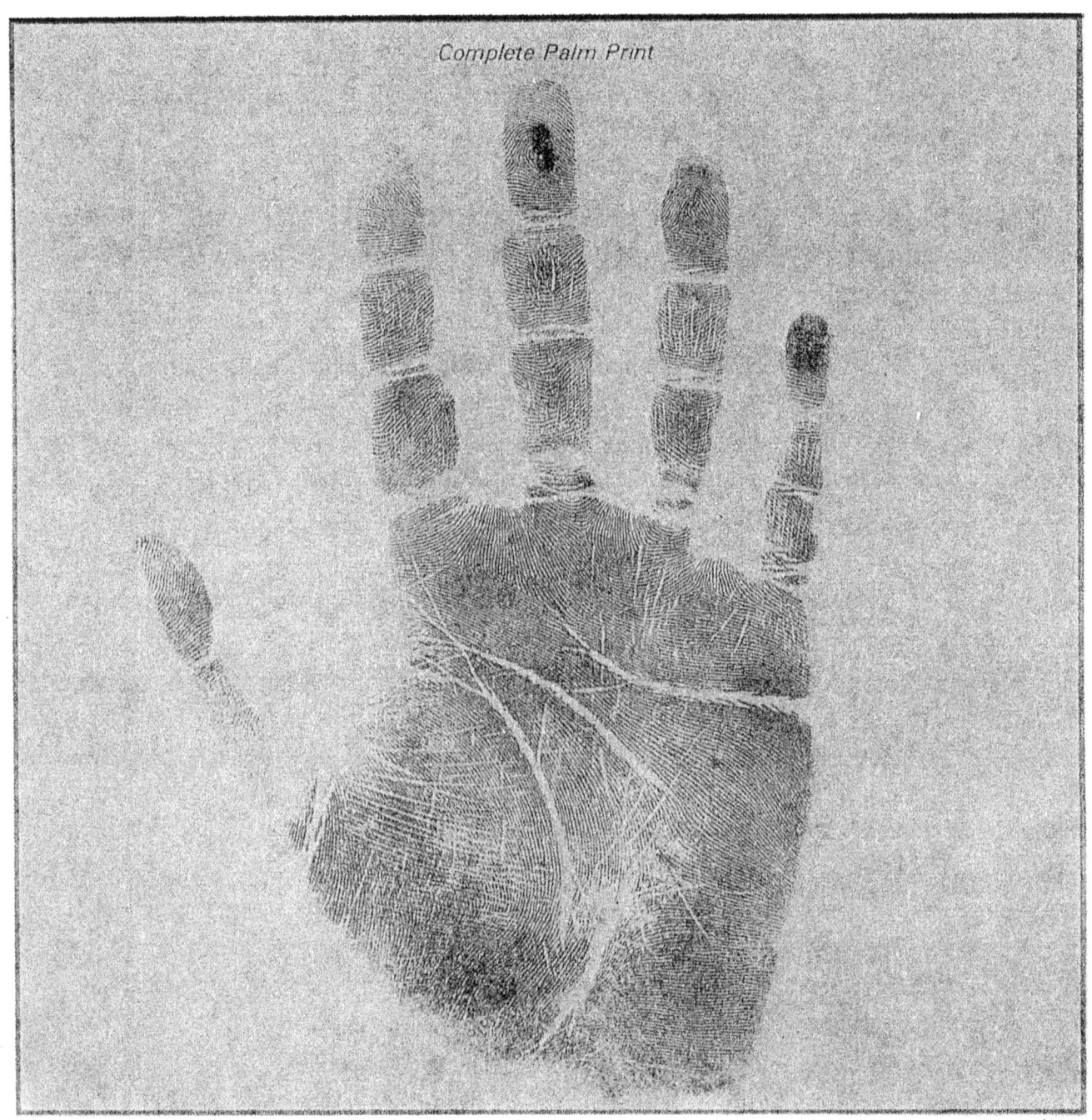

24   Back of SSF 1793 (Complete Right Palm)

CONCLUSION

Palmprint evidence can be a most important asset to an investigation. As with all types of physical evidence, the results of technical examinations are directly related to the proper collection and recording of the evidence by the investigator. Adherence to the procedures set forth should produce inked palmprint impressions that lend themselves to a thorough technical examination.